Japanese for Fun

Japanese for Fun

Make Your Stay in Japan More Enjoyable!

Taeko Kamiya

Tuttle Publishing

Boston, Rutland, Vermont, Tokyo

Published by Tuttle Publishing
an imprint of Periplus Editions (HK) Limited

LCC Card No. 89-51718
ISBN 0-8048-1628-X

First edition, 1990
Ninth printing, 2001

Printed in Singapore

Distributed by:

North America
Tuttle Publishing
 Distribution Center, Airport Industrial Park
 364 Innovation Drive
 North Clarendon, VT 05759-9436
 Tel: (802) 773 8930
 Fax: (802) 773 6993

Japan & Korea
 Tuttle Publishing
 RK Bldg, 2nd Floor 2-13-10 Shimo-Meguro
 Meguro-ku Tokyo 153 0064
 Tel: (03) 5437 0171
 Fax: (03) 5437 0755

Asia-Pacific
 Berkeley Books Pte Ltd
 5 Little Road, #08-01
 Singapore 536983
 Tel: (65) 280 1330
 Fax: (65) 280 6290

Contents

Foreword

This pocket book is intended for people who want to learn Japanese quickly. Whenever you have a few free minutes—waiting in a hotel lobby, riding on a train, or wherever—open this book and you can learn phrases you'll use again and again during your stay in Japan.

The book is divided into twenty-one chapters, each covering a specific topic. Each chapter includes the following three sections.

Words & Expressions: This section introduces words and expressions needed in specific situations. Vocabulary is presented systematically for quick and easy understanding.

Expressions in Context: This shows how to use in context the words and expressions given in the preceding section. Gives you confidence in using new words in original sentences.

Additional Words & Expressions: This section enables you to create many new sentences using the patterns just learned. There's no need to memorize all the words or phrases presented here; concentrate on just those you want to use.

Start by reading the first three chapters of the book. These introduce many of the most commonly used words and phrases, and familiarize you with the basic sentence structures. After Chapter 3, go straight to any chapter that interests you. If you want to know what to say on the phone, read Chapter 14; if you have to take a train, a few minutes with Chapter 6 should enable you to reach your destination quickly and conveniently.

Altogether, this book contains over three hundred carefully selected words and expressions. There is very little grammar included and there is no need for hours of rote memorization. All that is required is a few minutes of your time.

One final word of advice. Do not be afraid to use what you learn. Only by taking the initiative and speaking out can you experience the joy of communicating in a foreign language. With this new method, you'll discover how fun and easy speaking Japanese can be.

The Author

Pronunciation

Vowels

The Japanese language has five vowels: *a, i, u, e,* and *o.* The vowels are pronounced as follows:

a	as in f*a*ther
i	as in *ea*t
u	as in r*u*le
e	as in m*e*t
o	as in s*o*lo

In spoken Japanese, the *i* and *u* vowel sounds are often weak. This occurs in words like *shika* (deer), which may sound like *shka,* or *desu,* which may sound like *des.*

Long vowels are pronounced twice as long as regular vowels and are marked *ā, ii* or *ī, ū, ē,* and *ō.* In this book the double *ii* is used instead of a macron.

Consonants

Most Japanese consonants are pronounced like English consonants. One exception is the Japanese *r,* which sounds like a combination of the English *r* and *l.*

As shown in the following table, each consonant is followed by a vowel, by a *y* and a vowel, or by an *h* and a vowel. Each syllable is clearly pronounced; thus *haru* (spring) is *ha-ru;* *kyaku* (customer) is *kya-ku*; and *shumi* (hobby) is *shu-mi*.

When *n* is followed by a vowel within a word, an apostrophe is used to show the break between syllables. Examples of this include *kin'en* (nonsmoking) and *man'in* (no vacancy).

Double consonants *(kk, pp, ss, tt)* are pronounced as follows: *Nikko* (famous tourist spot) like the *k* sound in "book-keeper"; *rippa* (fine) like the *p* sound in "top *p*art"; *issō* (more) like the *s* sound in "less *s*leep"; *kitte* (stamp) like the *t* sound in "hot *t*ub."

Following is a table of all the sounds in Japanese. It is recommended that you practice the sounds aloud at least two or three times.

Table of Sounds in Japanese

a	*i*	*u*	*e*	*o*
ka	*ki*	*ku*	*ke*	*ko*
ga	*gi*	*gu*	*ge*	*go*
sa	*shi*	*su*	*se*	*so*
za	*ji*	*zu*	*ze*	*zo*
ta	*chi*	*tsu*	*te*	*to*
*tsa**	*ti**	*tu**	*tse**	*tso**
da	*di**	*du**/*dyu**	*de*	*do*
na	*ni*	*nu*	*ne*	*no*
ha	*hi*	*fu*	*he*	*ho*
ba	*bi*	*bu*	*be*	*bo*
pa	*pi*	*pu*	*pe*	*po*
*fa**	*fi**	—	*fe**	*fo**
ma	*mi*	*mu*	*me*	*mo*

ya	—	yu	—	yo
ra	ri	ru	re	ro
wa	—	—	—	—
n	—	—	—	—
kya	—	kyu	—	kyo
gya	—	gyu	—	gyo
sha	—	shu	she*	sho
ja	—	ju	je*	jo
cha	—	chu	che*	cho
nya	—	nyu	—	nyo
hya	—	hyu/fyu*	—	hyo
bya	—	byu	—	byo
pya	—	pyu	—	pyo
mya	—	myu	—	myo
rya	—	ryu	—	ryo

*These sounds are used only in loanwords, words derived from other languages.

A Word About
Japanese Grammar

It is not the purpose of this book to explain Japanese grammar. However, it is probably worthwhile to point out a few basic differences between Japanese and English.

1. Japanese verbs come at the end of a sentence.
    Ex. *Watashi wa biiru o <u>nomimasu</u>.* (I <u>drink</u> beer.)

2. Japanese nouns generally do not have plural forms. The noun *kodomo*, for example, can mean either "child" or "children."

3. Articles and some common English adjectives are not used in Japanese. There are no Japanese equivalents for words like "a," "the," "some," and "any."

4. The subject of a sentence, especially *watashi* (I) and *anata* (you), is often dropped.

5. The same verb form is used for both the present and future tenses.
    Ex. *Watashi wa ikimasu.* (I go./I will go.)

6. Three important Japanese particles have no equivalents in English.

   Wa follows the topic or subject of a sentence.
   Ex. *Watashi wa Honda desu.* (I am Honda.)
   Ga follows the subject of a sentence.
   Ex. *Hoteru ga arimasu.* (There is a hotel.)
   O follows the direct object of a verb.
   Ex. *Biiru o nomimasu.* (I drink beer.)

7. Adding the word *ka* to the end of a sentence makes it a question.
   Ex. *Kore wa hoteru desu ka?* (Is this a hotel?)

Basic Expressions

You'll use these basic expressions again and again during your stay in Japan. If you can, practice them aloud. It'll take you only a few moments to learn them, and when you do, you'll have taken the first and most important step to speaking Japanese.

Words & Expressions

Ohayō gozaimasu.	Good morning.
Konnichiwa.	Hello. / Good afternoon.
Konbanwa.	Good evening.
Oyasumi-nasai.	Good night.
Sayōnara.	Goodbye.
Jā mata.	See you later.
Omedetō gozaimasu.	Congratulations.
Dōmo arigatō.	Thank you.
Dō-itashimashite.	You're welcome.
O-genki desu ka?	How are you?
o-	(honorific prefix)
genki	healthy; fine
hai	yes
iie	no
Hai, genki desu.	(Yes,) I'm fine.

Hajimemashite.	How do you do? (used only when you are introduced to someone)
Dōzo yoroshiku.	Glad to meet you.
O-namae wa?	What's your name?
O-shigoto wa?	What's your occupation?
Wakarimasu.	I understand.
Wakarimasen.	I don't understand.
Nihon-go	Japanese (language)
Nihon-go wa wakarimasen.	I don't understand Japanese.
Nihon-go ga heta desu.	My Japanese is poor.
Sumimasen.	Excuse me.
Honda-san	Mr./Mrs./Ms./Miss Honda
-san	(honorific added to another person's name; not used with your own name)
Ei-go	English
Ei-go ga wakarimasu ka?	Do you understand English?

How to Bow

Bowing properly takes practice, and many companies, especially hotels and department stores, spend considerable time training new employees to do it correctly. The secret to good bowing? Keep your back straight and bend from the hip. Your feet should be placed together and your hands at your sides or clasped in front. Bow deliberately, without rushing. If you don't know what to say as you bow, say *Dōmo*, a phrase that's appropriate for most occasions. One exception is when you're paying respects to the deceased. In that case, just keep silent.

Expressions in Context

Honda-san, konnichiwa.	Good afternoon, Mr. Honda.
Sumisu-san, konnichiwa.	Good afternoon, Mrs. Smith.
Sumisu-san, ohayō gozaimasu.	Good morning, Mr. Smith.
Sumisu-san, konbanwa.	Good evening, Miss Smith.
O-genki desu ka?	How are you?
Hai, genki desu.	(Yes,) I'm fine.
Hajimemashite. Honda desu. Dōzo yoroshiku.	How do you do? I'm Honda. I'm glad to meet you.
Hajimemashite. Sumisu desu. Dōzo yoroshiku.	How do you do? I'm Smith. I'm pleased to meet you.
Omedetō gozaimasu.	Congratulations!
Dōmo arigatō.	Thank you.
Dō-itashimashite.	You're welcome.
Jā mata.	See you later.
Sayōnara.	Goodbye.
Oyasumi-nasai.	Good night.

Additional Words & Expressions

Wakarimasu ka?	Do you understand?
Hai, wakarimasu.	Yes, I understand.
Iie, wakarimasen.	No, I don't understand.
Mō ichido itte kudasai.	Please say it once more.
Ei-go de hanashite kudasai.	Please speak in English.
yukkuri	slowly
Yukkuri hanashite kudasai.	Please speak slowly.

LANGUAGES

Betonamu-go	Vietnamese
Chūgoku-go	Chinese
Doitsu-go	German
Furansu-go	French
Indoneshia-go	Indonesian
Itaria-go	Italian
Kankoku-go	Korean
Porutogaru-go	Portuguese
Roshia-go	Russian
Supein-go	Spanish
Tai-go	Thai

What's What

Over half of what we say in English is made up of fewer than fifty words. It's the same in Japanese. Just by learning the following words and phrases, you'll be able to make hundreds of different sentences. And remember, to make a question, add *ka* to the end of a sentence.

Words & Expressions

kore	this
wa	(subject particle)
jinja	Shinto shrine
desu	is; am; are
Kore wa jinja desu.	This is a Shinto shrine.
are	that
o-tera	Buddhist temple
o-	(honorific prefix)
Are wa o-tera desu.	That is a Buddhist temple.
Kabuki-za	the Kabuki Theater
kabuki	Kabuki
Are wa Kabuki-za desu ka?	Is that the Kabuki Theater?
hai	yes
sō desu	that's right
Hai, sō desu.	Yes, it is.

iie	no
dewa arimasen	isn't; am not; aren't
hanga	woodblock print
Kore wa hanga dewa arimasen.	This isn't a woodblock print.
nan(i)	what
Kore wa nan desu ka?	What's this?
torii	Shinto shrine archway
Torii desu.	This is a Shinto shrine archway.
Kōkyo	the Imperial Palace
Kore wa Kōkyo desu ka?	Is this the Imperial Palace?
o-shiro	castle
Are wa o-shiro desu ka?	Is that a castle?
bonsai	miniature potted tree or shrub
Kore wa bonsai desu.	This is a *bonsai.*
fūrin	wind chime
Are wa fūrin dewa arimasen.	That isn't a wind chime.

Shrines and Temples

What's the difference between a shrine and a temple? Shrines are worship grounds for Shinto, a religion that originated in Japan. Temples are worship grounds for Buddhism, which originally came from India. In many places in Japan, shrines and temples stand side by side.

A shrine can be identified by a *torii,* an arch made of two crossbeams supported by two pillars. The *torii* represents the union of man and woman and marks the entrance to the shrine grounds. At a temple, you can always find a statue of a buddha inside one of the buildings.

Expressions in Context

Kore wa nan desu ka?	What's this?
O-tera desu.	This is a Buddhist temple.
Kore wa jinja desu.	This is a Shinto shrine.
Kore wa torii desu.	This is a Shinto shrine archway.
Are wa nan desu ka?	What's that?
Are wa Kabuki-za desu.	That's the Kabuki Theater.
Are wa Kōkyo desu.	That's the Imperial Palace.
Are wa o-shiro desu.	That's a castle.
Kore wa hanga desu ka?	Is this a woodblock print?
Hai, sō desu.	Yes, it is.
Iie, hanga dewa arimasen.	No, it's not a woodblock print.
Kore wa bonsai desu ka?	Is this a *bonsai?*
Hai, sō desu.	Yes, it is.
Iie, bonsai dewa arimasen.	No, it's not a *bonsai.*
Are wa fūrin desu ka?	Is that a wind chime?
Iie, fūrin dewa arimasen.	No, it isn't a wind chime.

Additional Words & Expressions

GEOGRAPHICAL TERMS

yama	mountain
heiya	plain; open field
kawa	river
mizuumi	lake
umi	ocean
Taihei-yō	Pacific Ocean
Seto-naikai	Inland Sea
ken	prefecture
Hiroshima Ken	Hiroshima Prefecture

SIGHTSEEING

machi	town; city
inaka	country; rural area
tō	pagoda; tower
butsuzō	statue of a buddha
sanmon	temple gate
hakubutsu-kan	museum
bijutsu-kan	art museum
dōbutsu-en	zoo
shokubutsu-en	botanical garden
yūen-chi	amusement park
Ueno Kōen	Ueno Park
eki	station
Tōkyō Eki	Tokyo Station
Tōkyō Tawā	Tokyo Tower
Teikoku Hoteru	Imperial Hotel
cha-batake	tea field
kaki-yōshokujō	oyster bed (cultivated)
suiden	rice paddy

AROUND TOWN

dōro	road
kōsoku-dōro	expressway
michi	street
biru	building
kōsō-biru	skyscraper
hoteru	hotel

Introducing Yourself

Polite speech in Japanese, which is very complicated, is based on being respectful when referring to others and humble when referring to yourself. Don't worry about polite speech too much though. Just remember to attach -san to other people's names and to not use it with yours.

Words & Expressions

watashi	I
Sumisu	Smith
desu	is; am; are
Watashi wa Sumisu desu.	My name is Smith. (*lit.*, I'm Smith.)
Amerika-jin	American (person)
Watashi wa Amerika-jin desu.	I'm an American.
anata	you
Tanaka-san	Mr./Mrs./Ms./Miss Tanaka
ka	(question particle)
Anata wa Tanaka-san desu ka?	Are you Mr. Tanaka?
Sō desu.	That's right.
Chigaimasu.	No, I'm not.
dewa arimasen	isn't; am not; are not
Nihon-jin	Japanese (person)

ano	that
hito	person
ano hito	that person
dare	who
Ano hito wa dare desu ka?	Who's that person?
watashi no	my
chichi	father (one's own father)
Watashi no chichi desu.	He's my father.
Tanaka-san no	Mr./Mrs./Ms./Miss Tanaka's
otōsan	father (someone else's father; also used when addressing one's own father)
Tanaka-san no otōsan desu.	He's Mrs. Tanaka's father.
anata no	your
namae	name
Anata no namae wa?	What's your name?

Polite Complications

Many new employees spend their first days on the job learning when to use honorific and humble speech. It can be confusing at first. For example, suppose a new employee is talking to the company president. He'll be using as many honorifics as he can. The phone rings. The young man picks it up but it's for the president. "He's in" the young man says using humble speech to refer to his president. Rude? Far from it. He's merely showing respect to the caller, someone outside his company, by using humble speech to refer to a member of his own company, even if that person's status is much higher than his.

Expressions in Context

Ano hito wa dare desu ka?	Who's that person?
Tanaka-san desu.	That's Mr. Tanaka.
Watashi wa Sumisu desu.	My name is Smith.
Watashi wa Amerika-jin desu.	I'm an American.
Anata wa Sumisu-san desu ka?	Are you Miss Smith?
Hai, sō desu.	Yes, I'm.
Iie, chigaimasu.	No, I'm not.
Anata wa Amerika-jin desu ka?	Are you an American?
Anata wa Nihon-jin desu ka?	Are you Japanese?
Ano hito wa Tanaka-san no otōsan desu ka?	Is that person Mrs. Tanaka's father?
Watashi wa Nihon-jin dewa arimasen.	I'm not Japanese.
Ano hito wa Tanaka-san dewa arimasen.	That person isn't Mr. Tanaka.
Ano hito wa watashi no chichi dewa arimasen.	That person isn't my father.
Anata no namae wa?	What's your name?
Sumisu desu.	My name is Smith.

Additional Words & Expressions

NATIONS AND NATIONALITIES

Amerika	United States
Betonamu	Vietnam
Betonamu-jin	Vietnamese
Chūgoku	China
Chūgoku-jin	Chinese
Furansu	France
Furansu-jin	French
Igirisu	England
Igirisu-jin	English
Itaria	Italy
Itaria-jin	Italian
Kanada	Canada
Kanada-jin	Canadian
Kankoku	Korea (ROK)
Kankoku-jin	Korean
Nishi Doitsu	West Germany
Doitsu-jin	German
Ōsutoraria	Australia
Ōsutoraria-jin	Australian
Porutogaru	Portugal
Porutogaru-jin	Portuguese
Roshia	Russia
Roshia-jin	Russian
Supein	Spain
Supein-jin	Spanish

OCCUPATIONS

sensei	teacher
gakusei	student

hisho	secretary
kaisha-in	company employee
bengo-shi	lawyer
kisha	reporter; journalist

RELATIVES

haha	mother (one's own mother)
okāsan	mother (someone else's mother, and when addressing one's own mother)
ani	older brother (one's own older brother)
oniisan	older brother (someone else's older brother, and when addressing one's own older brother)
ane	older sister (one's own older sister)
onēsan	older sister (someone else's older sister, and when addressing one's own older sister)
otōto	younger brother (one's own younger brother)
otōto-san	younger brother (someone else's younger brother)
imōto	younger sister (one's own younger sister)
imōto-san	younger sister (someone else's younger sister)

musuko	son (one's own son)
musuko-san	son (someone else's son)
musume	daughter (one's own daughter)
musume-san	daughter (someone else's daughter)
mago	grandchild (one's own grandchild)
o-mago-san	grandchild (someone else's grandchild)

OTHERS

tomodachi	friend
kare	he
kanojo	she
kodomo	child
otona	adult
onna	female
otoko	male
onna no ko	girl
otoko no ko	boy
onna no hito	woman
otoko no hito	man

4

Asking Directions

With one word, *sumimasen,* you can ask a stranger a question, get a store clerk's attention, and apologize for just about anything. On top of that, you can use *sumimasen* to express thanks for a kind act; for example, when someone gives you directions or offers you something to drink.

Words & Expressions

Sumimasen.	Excuse me.
takushii-noriba	taxi stand
doko	where
Takushii-noriba wa doko desu ka?	Where's a taxi stand?
asoko	over there; that place
Asoko desu.	It's over there.
koko	here; this place
Koko wa doko desu ka?	Where am I?/Where's this place?
eki	station
tōi	far
Eki wa tōi desu ka?	Is the station far?
chikai	near
Iie, chikai desu.	No, it's near.

Shinjuku	Shinjuku (place name in Tokyo)
chizu	map
chizu de	on the map
Shinjuku wa chizu de doko desu ka?	Where on the map is Shinjuku?
o-tearai	restroom
O-tearai wa doko desu ka?	Where's the restroom?
soba	near
erebētā	elevator
Erebētā no soba desu.	It's near the elevator.
kusuri-ya	pharmacy
koko massugu	straight ahead
Kusuri-ya wa koko massugu desu ka?	Is the pharmacy straight ahead?
mae	in front
Hai, eki no mae desu.	Yes, it's in front of the station.

Speaking English in Japan

What to do when your Japanese fails you? Speak in English. English-speaking people abound in Japan—the trick is knowing who and how to ask. Your best bet lies with young businessmen, professional working women, and high school and college students. Many students, having spent years studying English, would love the chance to talk with you.

Still, when confronted by a foreigner, some Japanese may be so surprised that their hearing and speaking ability fail. Speak slowly and clearly. If that fails, try writing down what you want on paper.

Expressions in Context

O-tearai wa doko desu ka?	Where's a restroom?
Erebētā wa doko desu ka?	Where's an elevator?
Shinjuku wa tōi desu ka?	Is Shinjuku far?
Hai, tōi desu.	Yes, it's far.
Iie, chikai desu.	No, it's near.
Eki wa chizu de doko desu ka?	Where on the map is the station?
Koko desu.	Here it is.
Kusuri-ya wa eki no mae desu.	The pharmacy is in front of the station.
O-tearai wa erebētā no soba desu.	The restroom is near the elevator.
Takushii-noriba wa koko massugu desu.	The taxi stand is straight ahead.
Sumimasen. Koko wa doko desu ka?	Excuse me. Where am I?
Shinjuku desu.	In Shinjuku.
Eki wa chikai desu ka?	Is the station near?
Hai, asoko desu.	Yes, it's over there.

Additional Words & Expressions

PLACES

kūkō	airport
basu-tei	bus stop
chika-tetsu no eki	subway station
chūsha-jō	parking lot
gasorin-sutando	gas station
kyōkai	church
taishi-kan	embassy
ryōji-kan	consulate
ginkō	bank
yūbin-kyoku	post office
mise	store
depāto	department store
hon-ya	bookstore
kamera-ya	camera shop
pan-ya	bakery
gifuto-shoppu	gift shop
kissa-ten	coffee shop
keisatsu-sho	police station
kōban	police box

WITHIN A BUILDING

esukarētā	escalator
kaidan	stairs
kai	floor
Nan-kai desu ka?	What floor?
Ni-kai desu.	The second floor.
uketsuke	reception desk
naka	in; inside
soto	out; outside

chika	basement
okujō	roof
iriguchi	entrance
deguchi	exit

DIRECTIONS

higashi	east
nishi	west
kita	north
minami	south
ushiro	behind
ue	up
shita	down
migi	right
hidari	left

5

Numbers

For counting ten objects or less, use the numbers presented below. For example, if you want six rolls of film, say *Firumu, muttsu kudasai*. If you have four baggage pieces, say *Nimotsu ga yottsu arimasu*. The good thing about numbers is that you can always use your fingers to make certain someone understands you.

Words & Expressions

hitotsu	one
kudasai	please; please give
Hitotsu kudasai.	Please give me one.
kore	this
Kore, hitotsu kudasai.	Please give me one of this.
sandoitchi	sandwich
futatsu	two
Sandoitchi, futatsu kudasai.	Please give me two sandwiches.
firumu	film
mittsu	three
Firumu, mittsu kudasai.	Please give me three rolls of film.

yottsu	four
itsutsu	five
muttsu	six
nanatsu	seven
yattsu	eight
kokonotsu	nine
tō	ten
ikutsu	how many
Ikutsu desu ka?	How many are there?/How many do you want?
Tō desu.	There are ten./I want ten.
nimotsu	bag; baggage
ga	(subject particle)
arimasu	there is; there are
Nimotsu ga ikutsu arimasu ka?	How many bags are there?
Yottsu arimasu.	There are four.
takusan	many
Takusan arimasu.	There are many.

Counters

Another way of counting uses special words that are attached to numerals. These words, called counters, vary according to the type of object. For example, long, thin objects like pens take the counter *hon*; flat objects use *mai*.

Counters exist for cars, fish, birds, buildings, airplanes, clothing, small animals, and large animals. There's even one for Japanese poems, and a different one for Chinese poems. But don't fret about remembering all of them. It's all right to count things with *hitotsu, futatsu, mittsu,* etc.

Expressions in Context

Sumimasen. Kore, kudasai.	Excuse me. Please give me this.
Ikutsu desu ka?	How many do you want?
Tō, kudasai.	Ten, please.
Kore, futatsu kudasai.	Please give me two of these.
Kore, muttsu kudasai.	Please give me six of these.
Sandoitchi, yottsu kudasai.	Please give me four sandwiches.
Firumu, mittsu kudasai.	Please give me three rolls of film.
Firumu, itsutsu kudasai.	Please give me five rolls of film.
Nimotsu ga ikutsu arimasu ka?	How many bags are there?
Nanatsu arimasu.	There are seven.
Kokonotsu arimasu.	There are nine.
Firumu ga takusan arimasu ka?	Do you have many rolls of film?
Hai, yattsu arimasu.	Yes, I have eight.
Iie, hitotsu arimasu.	No, I have one.

Additional Words & Expressions

NUMBERS

The numbers presented here are used for time, prices, rankings, and so forth. These numbers may also be used for counting more than ten objects.

ichi	1
ni	2
san	3
shi/yon	4
go	5
roku	6
shichi/nana	7
hachi	8
ku/kyū	9
jū	10
jū-ichi	11
jū-ni	12
jū-san	13
jū-shi/jū-yon	14
jū-go	15
jū-roku	16
jū-shichi/jū-nana	17
jū-hachi	18
jū-ku/jū-kyū	19
ni-jū	20
ni-jū-ichi	21
san-jū	30
san-jū-ichi	31
yon-jū	40
go-jū	50

roku-jū	60
shichi-jū/nana-jū	70
hachi-jū	80
kyū-jū	90
hyaku	100
hyaku-ichi	101
hyaku-jū	110
ni-hyaku	200
san-byaku	300
yon-hyaku	400
go-hyaku	500
rop-pyaku	600
nana-hyaku	700
hap-pyaku	800
kyū-hyaku	900
sen	1,000
san-zen	3,000
has-sen	8,000
ichi-man	10,000
san-man	30,000
jū-man	100,000
hyaku-man	1,000,000

Firumu, jū-san kudasai.	Please give me thirteen rolls of film.
Kore, ni-jū kudasai.	Please give me twenty of these.

COUNTING PEOPLE

hitori	1 person
futari	2 people

-nin	(suffix used for counting more than two people)
san-nin	3 people
yo-nin	4 people
go-nin	5 people
roku-nin	6 people
shichi-nin / nana-nin	7 people
hachi-nin	8 people
kyū-nin / ku-nin	9 people
jū-nin	10 people
Hito ga go-nin imasu.	There are five people.
otoko no hito	man
onna no hito	woman

6

Taking the Trains

If you don't know which train ticket to buy, ask a station employee (or a kind-looking stranger). Or buy the cheapest ticket and pay the remainder when you get off. Make sure you ask which platform to use and which train to take; some trains don't stop at every station.

Words & Expressions

kono	this
densha	train
kono densha	this train
Ōsaka	Osaka
e	(particle indicating direction)
Ōsaka e	to Osaka
ikimasu	go
Kono densha wa Ōsaka e ikimasu ka?	Does this train go to Osaka?
ikimasen	doesn't go/don't go
Iie, ikimasen.	No, it doesn't go.
-yuki	bound for ~
Ōsaka-yuki	bound for Osaka
dore	which one

Ōsaka-yuki wa dore desu ka?	Which one is bound for Osaka?
are	that one
Are desu.	That one is.
kippu	ticket
ikura	how much
Kippu wa ikura desu ka?	How much is the ticket?
Kyōto	Kyoto
Kyōto made	to Kyoto; as far as Kyoto
Kyōto made, ikura desu ka?	How much is it to Kyoto?
Roppongi	Roppongi (place name in Tokyo)
Roppongi made, ikura desu ka?	How much is it to Roppongi?
dono	which
hōmu	platform
Dono hōmu desu ka?	Which platform is it?
san-ban	#3
san-ban hōmu	platform #3
San-ban hōmu desu.	It's platform #3.

Japan's Trains

Japan has perhaps the best train and subway system in the world. Not only are trains safe, clean, and efficient, they traverse practically every part of Japan. The Japan Railways Group (JR), which owns eighty percent of Japan's rail system, offers a handy, economical rail pass. With this pass, you can ride throughout Japan on JR trains (including the bullet trains) as well as on JR buses and ferries. Ask your travel agent how to purchase the pass before you leave your home country because you cannot buy it in Japan.

Expressions in Context

Sumimasen. Kono densha wa Ōsaka e ikimasu ka?	Excuse me. Does this train go to Osaka?
Hai, ikimasu.	Yes, it does.
Iie, ikimasen.	No, it doesn't.
Kyōto-yuki wa dore desu ka?	Which one is bound for Kyoto?
Roppongi-yuki wa are desu ka?	Is that one bound for Roppongi?
Tōkyō-yuki wa dono hōmu desu ka?	Which platform does the train bound for Tokyo leave from?
Kippu wa ikura desu ka?	How much is the ticket?
Ōsaka made, ikura desu ka?	How much is it to Osaka?
Tōkyō made, ikura desu ka?	How much is it to Tokyo?
Sumimasen. Kyōto-yuki wa are desu ka?	Excuse me. Is that one bound for Kyoto?
Iie. Yon-ban hōmu desu.	No. It leaves from platform #4.
Iie. Ōsaka-yuki desu.	No. It is bound for Osaka.

Additional Words & Expressions

TYPES OF TRAINS

Shinkansen	bullet train
tokkyū	limited express
kyūkō	express
futsū	local train
chika-tetsu	subway

AT THE STATION

te-nimotsu ichiji azukari-jo	baggage checkroom
kiosuku; eki no baiten	kiosk, newspaper stand, station shop
machiai-shitsu	waiting room
rokkā	locker
annai-jo	information office
unchin-hyō	fare table
jikoku-hyō	timetable
(kippu no) jidō-hanbaiki	ticket machine
kaisatsu-guchi	wicket; ticket gate
katamichi(-kippu)	one-way (ticket)
ōfuku(-kippu)	round-trip (ticket)
zaseki shitei-ken	reserved-seat ticket

ON THE PLATFORM

-gō-sha	car # ~
ni-gō-sha	car #2
~ -ban-sen	track # ~
Nan-ban-sen desu ka?	Which track # is it?
San-ban-sen desu.	It's track #3.
kin'en-sha	nonsmoking car
jiyū-seki	nonreserved seat

shitei-seki	reserved seat
Jiyū-seki wa nan-gō-sha desu ka?	Which cars have non-reserved seats?
shokudō-sha	dining car
eki-ben	box lunch sold at stations or on trains
akabō	redcap; porter
shashō	conductor
eki-in	station employee
nori-kae	transfer
Chūō-sen	Chuo line (train line from Tokyo to Nagano Prefecture)
-sen	line (train)
Tōkyō Eki de nori-kae desu ka?	Do I transfer at Tokyo Station?
Hai, Chūō-sen ni nori-kae desu.	Yes, you transfer to the Chuo line.
Chikatetsu ni nori-kae desu.	You transfer to the subway.

7

Buses and Taxis

If you can't find taxis on the street, you can usually get them at designated areas near train stations. Empty taxis display a red light; full ones, a green light. Try to have the address of your destination written in Japanese; this can be very helpful when riding taxis or buses.

Words & Expressions

Ginza	Ginza (place in Tokyo)
made	to; as far as
Ginza made	to Ginza
itte kudasai	please go
Ginza made itte kudasai.	Please go to Ginza.
migi e	to the right
magatte kudasai	please turn
Migi e magatte kudasai.	Please turn to the right.
hidari e	to the left
ano	that
kado	corner
ano kado de	at that corner
tomete kudasai	please stop (a car)
Ano kado de tomete kudasai.	Please stop at that corner.
toranku	trunk (of a car)

o	(direct object particle)
Toranku o akete kudasai.	Please open the trunk.
Kanda	Kanda (place name in Tokyo)
ni tomarimasu	stop at
basu	bus
Kono basu wa Kanda ni tomarimasu ka?	Does this bus stop at Kanda?
koko	here
tsuitara	when we get there
oshiete kudasai	please tell
Tsuitara, oshiete kudasai.	When we get there, please tell me.
ikura	how much
Ikura desu ka?	How much is it?
sen-en satsu	1,000-yen note
kuzushite kudasai	please break (into change)
Sen-en satsu, kuzushite kudasai.	Please break this 1,000-yen note.

Buses

In major cities, you usually pay a flat fee for riding a bus. Sometimes you pay when you get on, sometimes when you get off.

In smaller cities and rural areas, you usually pay according to the distance traveled. As you get on, look for a machine that automatically gives you a ticket with a number on it. This ticket, which indicates where you got on the bus, determines your fare. Hand over the ticket with your fare when you get off the bus. (If you get on at the terminal station, you don't get a ticket.)

Expressions in Context

Kanda made itte kudasai.	Please go to Kanda.
Ano kado made itte kudasai.	Please go to that corner.
Hidari e magatte kudasai.	Please turn to the left.
Toranku o akete kudasai.	Please open the trunk.
Sumimasen. Migi e magatte kudasai.	Excuse me. Please turn right.
Koko de tomete kudasai.	Please stop here.
Ikura desu ka?	How much is it?
Kono basu wa Ginza ni tomarimasu ka?	Does this bus stop at Ginza?
Hai, tomarimasu.	Yes, it does.
Iie.	No. (it doesn't)
Tsuitara, oshiete kudasai.	Please tell me when we get there.
Sumimasen. Kore, kuzushite kudasai.	Excuse me. Please break this.
Sen-en satsu, kuzushite kudasai.	Please break this 1,000-yen note.
Dōmo arigatō.	Thank you.

Additional Words & Expressions

TAXIS

takushii	taxi
kōsaten	intersection
Ano kōsaten de hidari e magatte kudasai.	Please turn left at that intersection.
shingō	traffic light
aka-shingō	red light
ao-shingō	green light
Oroshite kudasai.	Please let me out.
ryōshū-sho	receipt
Ryōshū-sho, kudasai.	Please give me a receipt.

BUSES

basu-tei	bus stop
Basu-tei wa doko desu ka?	Where's a bus stop?
buzā	buzzer (to indicate you want to get off)
san-ban basu	bus #3

OTHERS

fune	ship
ferii	ferry
yūran-sen	excursion boat
nori-ba	entrance to board; landing
kippu	ticket
Kippu wa ikura desu ka?	How much is the ticket?

Telling Time

To tell time, combine the numbers introduced on page 38 (*ichi, ni, san,* etc.) with *ji* (hour) and *fun* (minute). Remember that a.m. is *gozen,* and p.m. is *gogo.* These words go before the time, as in *gozen jū-ji* (10:00 a.m.). Note that in some cases, *fun* changes to *pun.*

Words & Expressions

ichi-ji	1:00
Ichi-ji desu.	It's 1:00.
gozen	a.m.
gogo	p.m.
yo-ji	4:00
Gogo yo-ji desu.	It's 4:00 p.m.
ip-pun	one minute
ni-fun	two minutes
san-pun	three minutes
yon-pun	four minutes
go-fun	five minutes
rop-pun	six minutes
shichi-fun / nana-fun	seven minutes
hachi-fun / hap-pun	eight minutes
kyū-fun	nine minutes

jup-pun	ten minutes
Gozen go-ji jup-pun desu.	It's 5:10 a.m.
mae	before
go-ji jup-pun mae	10 minutes before 5:00
han	half (past)
Gogo roku-ji-han desu.	It's 6:30 p.m.
ima	now
nan-ji	what time
Ima nan-ji desu ka?	What time is it now?
nan-ji ni	what time
dekakemasu	go out; leave
Nan-ji ni dekakemasu ka?	What time shall we go out?
asa-gohan	breakfast
Asa-gohan wa nan-ji desu ka?	What time is breakfast?
ban-gohan	supper
eiga	movie
hajimarimasu	start
Eiga wa nan-ji ni hajimarimasu ka?	What time does the movie start?

Time Information

Trains and planes operate on the 24-hour timetable. Thus, midnight is 00:00, 9 a.m. is 09:00, and 5 p.m. is 17:00. If this is confusing, confirm times using the regular 12-hour method, carefully enunciating *gozen* (a.m.) or *gogo* (p.m.).

All of Japan lies in a single time zone that is one hour behind Sydney, one hour ahead of Hong Kong, nine hours ahead of London, and fourteen hours ahead of New York. If you want to confirm the time in any major city, dial 0051. That number connects you with KDD, Japan's largest international telephone service. The operators speak English.

Expressions in Context

Ima nan-ji desu ka?	What time is it now?
Hachi-ji desu.	It's 8:00.
Ku-ji go-fun desu.	It's 9:05.
Jū-ji nana-fun mae desu.	It's 7 minutes before 10:00.
Ichi-ji san-jup-pun desu.	It's 1:30.
Ni-ji-han desu.	It's 2:30.
Gozen roku-ji ni-jū-go-fun desu.	It's 6:25 a.m.
Gogo yo-ji-han desu.	It's 4:30 p.m.
Ban-gohan wa nan-ji desu ka?	What time is supper?
Shichi-ji jū-go-fun desu.	It's at 7:15.
Eiga wa nan-ji desu ka?	What time is the movie?
San-ji yon-jū-go-fun desu.	It's at 3:45.
Nan-ji ni hajimarimasu ka?	What time does it start?
Go-ji ni-jup-pun desu.	At 5:20.
Kabuki wa nan-ji desu ka?	What time is the Kabuki performance?
Hachi-ji ni hajimarimasu.	It starts at 8:00.
Nan-ji ni dekakemasu ka?	What time shall we leave?
Shichi-ji-han ni dekakemasu.	We'll leave at 7:30.

Additional Words & Expressions

gohan	meal; cooked rice
hiru-gohan	lunch
o-cha no jikan	teatime
tōchaku-jikan	arrival time
shuppatsu-jikan	departure time
Shuppatsu-jikan wa nan-ji desu ka?	What time do we depart?
kaimaku-jikan	the time a performance starts
kaiten-jikan	opening hour of a store
heiten-jikan	closing hour of a store
shūgō-jikan	meeting time
kaisan-jikan	break-up time; the time a group disperses
yakusoku	promise; engagement; appointment
yakusoku no jikan	time set for an appointment
tokei	watch; clock
mezamashi-dokei	alarm clock
Mezamashi-dokei ga arimasu ka?	Do you have an alarm clock?

Days of the Week

The key to improving your Japanese is to use it every chance you get. Don't be embarrassed and don't get discouraged. One tip: avoid putting stress in your speech. You're much better off speaking in a monotone than stressing the wrong syllables.

Words & Expressions

kyō	today
Getsu-yōbi	Monday
Kyō wa Getsu-yōbi desu.	Today is Monday.
ashita	tomorrow
Ka-yōbi	Tuesday
Ashita wa Ka-yōbi desu.	Tomorrow is Tuesday.
Sui-yōbi	Wednesday
Moku-yōbi	Thursday
Kin-yōbi	Friday
Do-yōbi	Saturday
Nichi-yōbi	Sunday
kinō	yesterday

deshita	was; were
Kinō wa Nichi-yōbi deshita.	Yesterday was Sunday.
asatte	day after tomorrow
nan-yōbi	what day (of the week)
kankō	sightseeing
Kankō wa nan-yōbi desu ka?	What day is for sightseeing?
kekkon-shiki	wedding ceremony
hakuran-kai	exposition
pātii	party
Pātii wa nan-yōbi desu ka?	What day is the party?
Do-yōbi desu.	It's Saturday.
sōbetsu-kai	farewell party
pikunikku	picnic
kengaku-ryokō	field trip; tour of a factory, institution, etc.
yasumi	holiday; day off

Meanings of the Days of the Week

In Japanese, the days of the week derive from the world of nature. *Getsu-yōbi* (Monday), means "moon day"; *Ka-yōbi* (Tuesday), "fire day"; *Sui-yōbi* (Wednesday), "water day"; *Moku-yōbi* (Thursday) "wood day"; *Kin-yōbi* (Friday), "gold day"; *Do-yōbi* (Saturday) "soil day"; and *Nichi-yōbi* (Sunday), "sun day." Interestingly enough, our Sunday and Monday derive from the sun and moon as well, but here the similarity stops.

Expressions in Context

Kyō wa nan-yōbi desu ka?	What day is today?
Getsu-yōbi desu.	It's Monday.
Ashita wa nan-yōbi desu ka?	What day is tomorrow?
Kin-yōbi desu.	It's Friday.
Kekkon-shiki wa nan-yōbi desu ka?	What day is the wedding ceremony?
Asatte desu.	The day after tomorrow.
Hakuran-kai wa nan-yōbi desu ka?	What day is the exposition?
Moku-yōbi desu.	Thursday.
Pikunikku wa Do-yōbi desu ka?	Is the picnic on Saturday?
Iie, Ka-yōbi desu.	No, it's on Tuesday.
Kinō wa nan-yōbi deshita ka?	What day was yesterday?
Nichi-yōbi deshita.	It was Sunday.
Sōbetsu-kai wa nan-yōbi deshita ka?	What day was the farewell party?
Getsu-yōbi deshita.	It was Monday.
Yasumi wa nan-yōbi deshita ka?	What day did you take off from work?
Ka-yōbi deshita.	I took off Tuesday.
Kengaku-ryokō wa Sui-yōbi deshita ka?	Was the field trip on Wednesday?
Iie, Kin-yōbi deshita.	No, it was on Friday.

Additional Words & Expressions

DAYS AND WEEKS

ototoi	day before yesterday
mae no hi	previous day
tsugi no hi	next day
heijitsu	weekday
shūmatsu	weekend
saijitsu	national holiday
kyūka	day off from work
karendā	calendar
konshū	this week
raishū	next week
senshū	last week
sen-senshū	week before last

EVENTS

enkai	banquet
kakuteru-pātii	cocktail party
kangei-kai	welcome party
o-sōshiki	funeral
konsāto	concert
shiai	game; match
gorufu no konpe	golf tournament
yakyū no shiai	baseball game
hanabi	fireworks
hanabi-taikai	fireworks display

Days, Months, Years

Remembering the names of the months is simple in Japanese. Just combine numbers (see page 38) with *gatsu* (month). Thus, *Hachi-gatsu* is the eighth month, August; *Jū-ni-gatsu* is the twelfth month, December; and *Ichi-gatsu* is the first month, January.

Words & Expressions

kyō	today
tsuitachi	the 1st
Kyō wa tsuitachi desu.	Today is the 1st.
ashita	tomorrow
Ashita wa futsuka desu.	Tomorrow is the 2nd.
mikka	the 3rd
yokka	the 4th
itsuka	the 5th
muika	the 6th
nanoka	the 7th
nan-nichi	what day (of the month)
Nan-nichi desu ka?	What's the date?
tenran-kai	exhibition
Tenran-kai wa nan-nichi desu ka?	What's the date of the exhibition?

o-matsuri	festival
kongetsu	this month
Ichi-gatsu	January
Kongetsu wa Ichi-gatsu desu.	This month is January.
raigetsu	next month
Ni-gatsu	February
Raigetsu wa Ni-gatsu desu.	Next month is February.
San-gatsu	March
Shi-gatsu	April
Go-gatsu	May
Roku-gatsu	June
Shichi-gatsu	July
Hachi-gatsu	August
Ku-gatsu	September
Jū-gatsu	October
Jū-ichi-gatsu	November
Jū-ni-gatsu	December
Nan-gatsu desu ka?	What month is it?
Nan-gatsu nan-nichi desu ka?	What month and what day is it?

The Moon and the Months

Gatsu (month), a variant of *getsu* as in *Getsu-yōbi* (Monday), literally means "moon." The moon, as we know, became associated with months because it completes one cycle in a four-week period. You could think of the Japanese months as first moon, second moon, third moon, and so on.

Speaking of the moon, the Japanese have long celebrated "moon viewing." Called *tsuki-mi,* it was often a gathering of nobles and courtiers who relaxed on a veranda, gazed at the autumn moon, and composed short, poetic verses.

Expressions in Context

Kyō wa nan-nichi desu ka?	What's the date today?
Itsuka desu.	It's the 5th.
Ashita wa nan-nichi desu ka?	What's the date tomorrow?
Muika desu.	It's the 6th.
O-matsuri wa nan-nichi desu ka?	What's the date of the festival?
Tsuitachi desu.	It's the 1st.
Kongetsu wa nan-gatsu desu ka?	What month is this month?
Ichi-gatsu desu.	It's January.
Tenran-kai wa nan-gatsu desu ka?	What month is the exhibition?
Ni-gatsu desu.	It's February.
Tenran-kai wa raigetsu desu.	The exhibition is next month.
Kyō wa nan-gatsu nan-nichi desu ka?	What's the date today?
Roku-gatsu tsuitachi desu.	It's June 1st.
Ku-gatsu nanoka desu.	It's September 7th.
Tenran-kai wa nan-gatsu nan-nichi desu ka?	What's the date of the exhibition?
Raigetsu futsuka desu.	The 2nd of next month.

Additional Words & Expressions

DAYS OF THE MONTH

yōka	the 8th
kokonoka	the 9th
tōka	the 10th
jū-ichi-nichi	the 11th
jū-ni-nichi	the 12th
jū-san-nichi	the 13th
jū-yokka	the 14th
jū-go-nichi	the 15th
jū-roku-nichi	the 16th
jū-shichi-nichi	the 17th
jū-hachi-nichi	the 18th
jū-ku-nichi	the 19th
hatsuka	the 20th
ni-jū-ichi-nichi	the 21st
ni-jū-ni-nichi	the 22nd
ni-jū-san-nichi	the 23rd
ni-jū-yokka	the 24th
ni-jū-go-nichi	the 25th
ni-jū-roku-nichi	the 26th
ni-jū-shichi-nichi	the 27th
ni-jū-hachi-nichi	the 28th
ni-jū-ku-nichi	the 29th
san-jū-nichi	the 30th
san-jū-ichi-nichi	the 31st

YEARS

kotoshi	this year
kyonen	last year
ototoshi	year before last

rainen	next year
sarainen	year after next
mainen	every year
sen-kyū-hyaku kyū-jū-nen	1990
nan-nen	what year
Kotoshi wa nan-nen desu ka?	What year is this year?
Sen-kyū-hyaku kyū-jū-ichi-nen desu.	It's 1991.

OTHERS

kisetsu	season
haru	spring
natsu	summer
aki	autumn
fuyu	winter
mai-nichi	everyday
mai-ban	every night
sengetsu	last month
mai-getsu	every month
tanjō-bi	birthday
kinen-bi	anniversary

11

Asking About Times

Need to know when something will take place? For time, say *Nan-ji desu ka?* (What time is it/will it be?) and for dates, *Itsu desu ka?* (When is it?) When asking a stranger a question, remember to start off with *Sumimasen.* (For information about numbers, see Chapter 5.)

Words & Expressions

itsu	when
Kabuki wa itsu desu ka?	When is the Kabuki performance?
konban	tonight; this evening
Konban desu.	It's tonight.
shinai-kankō	tour of a city
nan-ji	what time
Shinai-kankō wa nan-ji desu ka?	What time is the city tour?
asa-gohan	breakfast
~ no ato (de)	after ~
Asa-gohan no ato desu.	It's after breakfast.
Kyūshū-meguri	tour of Kyushu
-meguri	tour of
ashita	tomorrow

Kyūshū-meguri wa ashita desu ka?	Is the Kyushu tour tomorrow?
Hai. Sō desu.	Yes, it is.
onsen	hot spring
onsen e	to a hot spring
Itsu onsen e ikimasu ka?	When will you go to the hot spring?
Konshū ikimasu.	I'll go this week.
hakubutsu-kan	museum
nan-yōbi	what day of the week
nan-yōbi ni	on what day of the week
Nan-yōbi ni hakubutsu-kan e ikimasu ka?	On what day will you go to the museum?
Do-yōbi ni	on Saturday
Do-yōbi ni ikimasu.	I'll go on Saturday.
ku-ji ni	at 9:00
Ku-ji ni ikimasu.	I'll go at 9:00.
tōka ni	on the 10th
Tōka ni ikimasu.	I'll go on the 10th.

Ni, E, and Wa

Here's some advice on how to use three important particles: *ni, e,* and *wa.* Use *ni* as you would "at" or "on" in a time-related expression like *"at* 9:30" *(ku-ji-han ni)* or "I go *on* the 10th" *(Tōka ni ikimasu).* For *e,* think of "to" when it refers to destinations, as in "I go *to* Tokyo" *(Tōkyō e ikimasu).* *Wa* has no corresponding English equivalent. In general, *wa* comes after the subject of a sentence, as in *Watashi wa Amerika-jin desu* (I'm American) or *Hoteru wa ii desu* (The hotel is nice). For now, whenever you say *watashi* (I), follow it with *wa.*

Expressions in Context

Itsu desu ka?	When is it?
Tōka desu.	It's on the 10th.
Do-yōbi desu.	It's on Saturday.
Shinai-kankō wa Getsu-yōbi desu ka?	Is the city tour on Monday?
Nan-ji desu ka?	What time will it be?
Asa-gohan no ato desu.	It's after breakfast.
Kyūshū-meguri wa itsu desu ka?	When is the Kyushu tour?
Konshū desu.	It's this week.
Tōka desu.	It's on the 10th.
Itsu onsen e ikimasu ka?	When will you go to the hot spring?
Konshū ikimasu.	I'll go this week.
Itsu hakubutsu-kan e ikimasu ka?	When will you go to the museum?
Asa-gohan no ato de ikimasu.	I'll go after breakfast.
Jū-ji ni ikimasu.	I'll go at 10:00.
Nan-yōbi ni ikimasu ka?	On what day will you go?
Konban ikimasu ka?	Will you go tonight?

Additional Words & Expressions

SCHEDULING

shokuji	meal
no mae (ni)	before
shokuji no mae	before a meal
ashita no asa	tomorrow morning
sugu	right away
mō sugu	soon; shortly
chikai uchi ni	one of these days
Chikai uchi ni ikimasu.	I'll go one of these days.
mai-shū	every week
raishū	next week
senshū	last week
natsu-yasumi	summer vacation
fuyu-yasumi	winter vacation
ryokō-sha	traveler
ryokō-sentā	travel bureau
dantai-ryokō	group tour
Dantai-ryokō de ikimasu.	I'll go with a group tour.
hitori	alone
Hitori de ikimasu.	I'll go by myself.
kaigai-ryokō	overseas travel
ryokō-hoken	travel insurance
gaido-bukku	guidebook

Talking About Food

If you plan to have a meal with Japanese people, you should master two phrases: *itadakimasu* and *gochisō-sama deshita*. Say *itadakimasu* before you start eating and *gochisō-sama deshita* when you have finished. All Japanese say these phrases at meals, and you'll leave a good impression if you do too.

Words & Expressions

o-cha	green tea
o	(direct object particle)
dōzo	please (do something)
O-cha o dōzo.	Please have some tea.
Itadakimasu.	Thank you. (I'll have some.)
Kekkō desu.	No, thank you.
o-kashi	sweets
ikaga	how about
O-kashi wa ikaga desu ka?	How about some sweets?
kore	this
nan(i)	what
Kore wa nan desu ka?	What's this?
o-manjū	(bun with bean-jam filling)
O-manjū desu.	It's a *manjū*.

naka	inside
Naka wa nan desu ka?	What's inside?
donna	what kind of
aji	taste
Donna aji desu ka?	What does it taste like?
amai	sweet
oishii	delicious
ne	isn't it?
Oishii desu ne.	It's delicious, isn't it?
Gochisō-sama deshita.	Thank you. (It was delicious.)
motto	more; some more
Motto ikaga desu ka?	How about some more?
o-naka	stomach
ga	(subject particle)
suite imasu	hungry
O-naka ga suite imasu.	I'm hungry.
ippai	full
O-naka ga ippai desu.	I'm full.
kukkii	cookie

Loanwords

Thousands of words in Japanese are loanwords, words derived from other languages. Try guessing the meanings of these drinks: *Koka-kōra, kōhii,* and *biiru.* Did you guess Coca-Cola, coffee, and beer? With exposure, you can easily increase your vocabulary just by learning loanwords.

Be careful, though, because not all loanwords come from English. For instance, *pan* (bread) comes from Portuguese, *ikura* (salmon roe) from Russian, and *arubaito* (part-time job) from German.

Expressions in Context

O-kashi o dōzo.	Please have some sweets.
Hai, itadakimasu.	Thank you.
Iie, kekkō desu.	No, thank you.
Kore wa nan desu ka?	What's this?
Naka wa nan desu ka?	What's inside?
Donna aji desu ka?	What does it taste like?
O-manjū wa ikaga desu ka?	How about a *manjū?*
Hai, itadakimasu.	Thank you.
Oishii desu ne.	Delicious, isn't it?
Amai desu ne.	Sweet, isn't it?
O-kashi wa oishii desu ne.	The sweets are delicious, aren't they?
Motto ikaga desu ka?	How about some more?
Iie, kekkō desu.	No, thank you.
O-naka ga ippai desu.	I'm full.
Gochisō-sama deshita.	Thank you. (It was wonderful.)
O-naka ga suite imasu.	I'm hungry.
Kukkii o dōzo.	Please have some cookies.
Itadakimasu.	Thank you. (I'll have some.)

Additional Words & Expressions

DESCRIBING FOOD

nama	raw
mazui	not tasty
atarashii	new; fresh
furui	old; stale
katai	hard; tough
yawarakai	soft; tender
atsui	hot
tsumetai	cold (to the touch)
karai	spicy
shoppai	salty
suppai	sour
nigai	bitter

DRINKS

mizu	water
kōhii	coffee
kōcha	black tea
biiru	beer
wain	wine
Koka-kōra	Coca-Cola
shōchū	(distilled spirit usually drunk with water or a mixer)
uisukii	whiskey
mizu-wari	whiskey and water

FRUIT

kuda-mono	fruit
ringo	apple

nashi	pear
momo	peach
budō	grape
mikan	tangerine
orenji	orange
suika	watermelon
meron	melon
kaki	persimmon

VEGETABLES

yasai	vegetable
retasu	lettuce
kyabetsu	cabbage
kabocha	pumpkin
tomato	tomato
jagaimo	potato
kyūri	cucumber
tōmorokoshi	corn
tamanegi	onion
nasu	eggplant
ninjin	carrot
shiitake	type of mushroom
renkon	lotus root
takenoko	bamboo shoot
sarada	salad

MEAT, SEAFOOD, POULTRY, DAIRY PRODUCTS

niku	meat
gyū-niku	beef
buta-niku	pork
sakana	fish

ebi	shrimp
ika	cuttlefish
tako	octopus
gyū-nyū	milk
yōguruto	yogurt
aisu-kuriimu	ice cream
tori-niku	chicken
tamago	egg

OTHERS

gohan	cooked rice (can also mean "meal")
raisu	rice (usually rice served with non-Japanese dishes)
tōfu	tofu
miso	miso (bean paste)
nori	seaweed
o-hashi	chopsticks
kēki	cake
senbei	rice cracker
Kore wa dō-yatte tabemasu ka?	How do you eat this?
nan de	with what
Kore wa nan de tabemasu ka?	What do you eat this with?

13

Dining Out

Travelers should not miss eating at a restaurant where the local residents are the main patrons. (Your hotel should know a good one nearby.) If you don't know what to order, try a set meal called a *teishoku*. Ask *Teishoku ga arimasu ka?* (Do you have set meals?) to find out if the restaurant serves them or not.

Words & Expressions

kono	this
hen	vicinity
kono hen ni	in this vicinity; around here
resutoran	restaurant
ga	(subject particle)
arimasu	there is; there are
Kono hen ni resutoran ga arimasu ka?	Is there a restaurant around here?
tenpura	tempura (deep-fried food)
wa	(subject particle, frequently used in negative sentences)
arimasen	don't have
Tenpura wa arimasen.	We don't have tempura.

nani	what
Nani ga arimasu ka?	What do you have?
o-nomimono	drink
O-nomimono wa?	How about a drink?
biiru	beer
o-negai shimasu	please (*lit.*, I make a request)
Biiru, o-negai shimasu.	Beer, please.
o-sake	saké (Japanese rice wine)
o-sushi	sushi (vinegared rice and raw fish)
kudasai	please give
O-sushi, kudasai.	Sushi, please.
Sumimasen.	Excuse me.
mizu	water
Sumimasen. Mizu, kudasai.	Excuse me. May I have some water?
karē-raisu	curry with rice
Karē-raisu, kudasai.	Curry with rice, please.
Kashikomarimashita.	Certainly, sir/ma'am.

Eating in Japanese Restaurants

Eating in Japan is a great experience. The food is good, healthy, and there's a great variety to choose from. But what if you can't read the menu? There's no need to worry, because many places have plastic food displays. Just take the waiter to the display case, and point to what you want to eat.

One tip for sushi lovers. If you don't know how to order sushi, call out *Nigiri-zushi, ichinin-mae!* and you'll get a tray of various types of sushi. You can also point, this time to the real thing, to other delicacies you want to try.

Expressions in Context

Kono hen ni resutoran ga arimasu ka?	Is there a restaurant around here?
Hai, arimasu.	Yes, there is.
Iie, arimasen.	No, there isn't.
Tenpura ga arimasu ka?	Do you have tempura?
Hai, arimasu.	Yes, we have.
Tenpura, o-negai shimasu.	Tempura, please.
Kashikomarimashita.	Certainly, sir.
Karē-raisu ga arimasu ka?	Do you have curry with rice?
Iie, karē-raisu wa arimasen.	No, we don't have curry with rice.
Nani ga arimasu ka?	What do you have?
Karē-raisu ga arimasu.	We have curry with rice.
O-sushi ga arimasu ka?	Do you have sushi?
Iie, o-sushi wa arimasen.	No, we don't have sushi.
O-nomimono wa?	How about a drink?
O-sake, kudasai.	Saké, please.
Mizu, o-negai shimasu.	Water, please.
Sumimasen. Biiru, kudasai.	Excuse me. Beer, please.

Additional Words & Expressions

MENU ITEMS

Nihon-ryōri	Japanese cuisine
Chūgoku-ryōri	Chinese cuisine
Seiyō-ryōri	Western cuisine
teishoku	set meal (includes main dish, soup, pickles, and rice)
gohan	rice
sui-mono	soup
tsuke-mono	pickle
suki-yaki	popular dish of meat, vegetable, bean curd, etc.
yaki-tori	grilled, skewered chicken
ton-katsu	pork cutlet
unagi-donburi	broiled eel and rice
udon	noodles (white and fat)
soba	buckwheat noodles (dark and thin)

TABLEWARE

chawan	rice bowl
yu-nomi	teacup
koppu	cup; glass
tokkuri	saké bottle
sakazuki	saké cup
sara	plate
o-hashi	chopsticks
o-shibori	hot or cold hand towel used to wipe one's hands before eating

fōku	fork
supūn	spoon
napukin	napkin

OTHERS

Kore wa dō-yatte tabemasu ka?	How do you eat this?
nan de	with what
Kore wa nan de tabemasu ka?	With what do you eat this?
o-kanjō	check
O-kanjō, o-negai shimasu.	May I please have the check?
Betsu-betsu ni, o-negai shimasu.	We'd like to pay separately.
Ikura desu ka?	How much is it?
kurejitto-kādo	credit card
Kurejitto-kādo de haraemasu ka?	May I pay with a credit card?
Oishii desu.	It's delicious.
Oishikatta desu.	It was delicious.

14

Making Telephone Calls

To use a public phone, put in a ten-yen coin, wait for a dial tone, and dial. If you're calling within your area code, you can speak three minutes for ten yen; the same amount will give you less time for calls outside your area code. Insert more if you need to talk longer. You'll receive your unused coins when you hang up.

Words & Expressions

Moshi-moshi.	Hello. (on the telephone)
o-negai shimasu	please
Yamada-san, o-negai shimasu.	Mr. Yamada, please. (May I speak with Mr. Yamada?)
shibaraku	a moment; awhile
o-machi kudasai	please wait
Shibaraku o-machi kudasai.	Please wait a moment.
Konnichiwa.	Hello./Good afternoon.
O-genki desu ka?	How are you?
Sumimasen ga...	Sorry, but...
ima	now
imasen	isn't in; aren't in
Sumimasen ga, Yamada wa ima imasen.	Sorry, but Mr. Yamada isn't in now.

dochira-sama	who
Dochira-sama desu ka?	Who is calling, please?
O-namae wa?	What's your name?
yoku	well
kikoemasen	can't hear
Yoku kikoemasen.	I can't hear well.
mō ichido	once more
itte kudasai	please say
Mō ichido itte kudasai.	Please say it once more.
Ei-go	English language
Ei-go de	in English
Ei-go de itte kudasai.	Please say it in English.
mata	again
o-denwa	telephone
o-denwa shimasu	make a telephone call
Mata o-denwa shimasu.	I'll call again.
Sayōnara.	Goodbye.

Telephones

The three most common types of public phones are red, yellow, and green phones. Red phones take only 10-yen coins, yellow telephones take 10-yen and 100-yen coins, and green telephones take telephone cards and usually 10-yen and 100-yen coins. Telephone cards come in denominations of 500 yen, 1,000 yen, and higher, and can be used instead of coins. You can purchase these telephone cards, available in a huge assortment of designs, at newsstands, vending machines, telephone offices, and convenience stores.

For helpful telephone services in English, refer to page 109.

Expressions in Context

Moshi-moshi. Yamada-san, o-negai shimasu.	Hello. May I speak to Mr. Yamada?
Hai. Shibaraku o-machi kudasai.	Yes. Please wait a moment.
Moshi-moshi. Yamada desu.	Hello. Yamada speaking.
Konnichiwa, Yamada-san. Buraun desu.	Hello, Mr. Yamada. This is Brown speaking.
Konnichiwa, Buraun-san. O-genki desu ka?	Hello, Mr. Brown. How are you?
Hai, arigatō. Genki desu.	Yes, I'm fine, thank you.
Sumimasen ga, yoku kikoemasen.	Excuse me, but I can't hear well.
Ei-go de mō ichido itte kudasai.	Please say it once more in English.
Moshi-moshi. Yamada-san wa imasu ka?	Hello. Is Mr. Yamada in?
Sumimasen ga, Yamada wa ima imasen.	Sorry, but he isn't in now.
Dochira-sama desu ka?	Who is calling, please?
Buraun desu. Mata o-denwa shimasu.	This is Brown. I'll call again.
Hai, o-negai shimasu.	Yes, please do.
Sayōnara.	Goodbye.

Additional Words & Expressions

denwa-bangō	telephone number
denwa-chō	telephone directory
denwa-ryō	telephone bill
kōshū-denwa	public telephone
shinai-denwa	local telephone call
chōkyori-denwa	long distance telephone call
kokusai-denwa	international telephone call
kōkan-shu	operator
korekuto-kōru	collect call
kurejitto-kādo	credit card
terefon-kādo	telephone card
messēji	message
Messēji wa o-negai dekimasu ka?	May I leave a message?
naisen	extension
bangō-chigai	wrong number
Bangō ga chigaimasu.	You have the wrong number.
O-denwa o karite mo ii desu ka?	May I use this phone?
O-denwa, dōmo arigatō.	Thank you for calling.
(O-)denwa wa doko desu ka?	Where's a phone?

15

Describing Your Plans

When you speak Japanese, use short, easy phrases. Try to simplify your language; for example, rather than trying to say "I intend to spend time looking at old Japanese Buddhist temples," say "I'll see temples." That becomes simply *O-tera o mimasu.*

Words & Expressions

ashita	tomorrow
Kyōto	Kyoto
Kyōto e	to Kyoto
ikimasu	go
Ashita Kyōto e ikimasu.	Tomorrow I'll go to Kyoto.
Kyōto de	in Kyoto; at Kyoto
nani	what
o	(object particle)
shimasu	do
Kyōto de nani o shimasu ka?	What will you do in Kyoto?
o-tera	Buddhist temple
mimasu	see
O-tera o mimasu.	I'll see temples.

82

yūmei na	famous
Yūmei na o-tera e ikimasu.	I'll go to a famous temple.
niwa	garden
Yūmei na niwa o mimasu.	I'll see famous gardens.
shashin	photo
torimasu	take
Shashin o torimasu.	I'll take some photos.
Kyōto de shashin o torimasu.	I'll take photos in Kyoto.
e-hagaki	postcard
kaimasu	buy
E-hagaki o kaimasu.	I'll buy some postcards.
O-tera de e-hagaki o kaimasu.	I'll buy some postcards at the temple.
o-miyage	souvenir
kōen	park
kōen made	to the park
arukimasu	walk
Kōen made arukimasu.	I'll walk to the park.

Enchanting Kyoto

Every visitor to Japan should experience wandering around Kyoto's back streets. Wherever you turn, you'll discover a myriad of shrines, temples, and traditional shops and residences. And in these back streets, you'll also find a peace and quiet that is rare in most other cities.

Because of its vast number of cultural treasures (there are over 400 shrines and 1,600 temples alone), Kyoto was not bombed in World War II. Thus, Kyoto remains Japan's cultural capital, a proud city that gave rise to one of the world's most refined civilizations.

Expressions in Context

Ashita Tōkyō e ikimasu.	I'll go to Tokyo tomorrow.
Ashita kōen e ikimasu.	I'll go to the park tomorrow.
Ashita yūmei na niwa e ikimasu.	I'll go to a famous garden tomorrow.
Kyōto de nani o mimasu ka?	What will you see in Kyoto?
Yūmei na niwa o mimasu.	I'll see famous gardens.
Nani o shimasu ka?	What will you do?
Kōen made arukimasu.	I'll walk to the park.
Kōen de shashin o torimasu.	I'll take some photographs in the park.
Nani o mimasu ka?	What will you see?
Yūmei na kōen o mimasu.	I'll see a famous park.
Kyōto de shashin o torimasu ka?	Will you take some photos in Kyoto?
Hai, torimasu.	Yes, I will.
Nani o kaimasu ka?	What will you buy?
O-miyage o kaimasu.	I'll buy some souvenirs.

Additional Words & Expressions

SPARE-TIME ACTIVITIES

zasshi	magazine
hon	book
shinbun	newspaper
Zasshi o yomimasu.	I'll read a magazine.
terebi	television
rajio	radio
Rajio o kikimasu.	I'll listen to the radio.
tegami	letter
Tegami o kakimasu.	I'll write a letter.
hoteru e	to the hotel
Hoteru e kaerimasu.	I'll return to the hotel.
orenji-jūsu	orange juice
Orenji-jūsu o nomimasu.	I'll drink orange juice.
hayaku	early
Hayaku okimasu.	I'll get up early.
osoku	late
Osoku nemasu.	I'll go to bed late.

16

Describing What You Did

If a Japanese word ends in *mashita,* you can be almost certain that it is a verb in its past tense. For example, the present tense of the verb "to go" is *ikimasu* and the past tense is *ikimashita.* The present tense of the verb "to do" is *shimasu* and the past tense is *shimashita.* There are few exceptions to this rule.

Words & Expressions

kinō	yesterday
doko	where
e	to
doko e	where to
ikimashita	went
Kinō doko e ikimashita ka?	Where did you go yesterday?
Nara	Nara
Nara e	to Nara
Nara e ikimashita.	I went to Nara.
Nara de	in Nara
nani	what
o	(object particle)
shimashita	did

Nara de nani o shimashita ka?	What did you do in Nara?
daibutsu	large statue of Buddha
mimashita	saw
Nara de daibutsu o mimashita.	I saw the large statue of Buddha in Nara.
kōen	park
arukimashita	walked
Kōen made arukimashita.	I walked to the park.
shashin	photograph
torimashita	took
Shashin o torimashita.	I took some photos.
shika	deer (Nara is famous for its deer.)
no	of
shika no shashin	photo of deer
o-miyage	souvenir
kaimashita	bought
O-miyage o kaimashita.	I bought souvenirs.

Origin of the Japanese Language

Where did the Japanese spoken language come from? No one knows for sure. Some feel there's a strong connection with the Altaic languages of Central Asia. Others believe Japanese derived from the languages of Southeast Asia and Polynesia. And a few insist that Japanese has no connections at all with any other language.

The writing system, on the other hand, came from China in the sixth century. At that time, Buddhism was being introduced from China, and a writing system was necessary to propagate the wisdom of the sutras.

Expressions in Context

Doko e ikimashita ka?	Where did you go?
Kyōto e ikimashita.	I went to Kyoto.
O-tera e ikimashita.	I went to a Buddhist temple.
Kōen e ikimashita.	I went to the park.
Nara de nani o mimashita ka?	What did you see in Nara?
O-tera o mimashita.	I saw Buddhist temples.
Kōen o mimashita.	I saw the park.
Shika o mimashita.	I saw deer.
Nani o shimashita ka?	What did you do?
Shashin o torimashita.	I took some photos.
Nani o mimashita ka?	What did you see?
O-tera o mimashita ka?	Did you see Buddhist temples?
Shashin o torimashita ka?	Did you take photos?
Hai, torimashita. Shika no shashin o torimashita.	Yes, I did. I took photos of the deer.
Nani o kaimashita ka?	What did you buy?
O-miyage o kaimashita.	I bought some souvenirs.

Additional Words & Expressions

daigaku	college; university
tosho-kan	library
eiga-kan	movie theater
gekijō	theater
garō	gallery
sutajiamu	stadium
hiro-ba	public square
shiseki	historical site
Shiseki e ikimashita.	I went to a historical site.
kinen-hi	monument
zō	statue
meisho	place of interest (tourist spots)
Kono hen ni meisho wa arimasu ka?	Are there any tourists spots around here?
meisan	regional specialty
Kono hen no meisan wa nan desu ka?	What product is this area famous for?
nyūjō-ken	admission ticket
Nyūjō-ken o kaimashita.	I bought an admission ticket.
nyūjō-ryō	admission fee
Nyūjō-ryō wa ikura desu ka?	How much is the admission fee?

Expressing What You Want

Remember that communicating is your objective. Don't worry if your particles are wrong or your word order is incorrect. If you're unsure about a particle, simply skip over it. The truth is that many Japanese drop particles in conversation, so it's not a problem if you do too.

Words & Expressions

Nihon ningyō	Japanese doll
ga	(subject particle)
hoshii	want
Nihon ningyō ga hoshii desu.	I want a Japanese doll.
ryokan	Japanese inn
suki	like
Ryokan ga suki desu.	I like Japanese inns.
hoteru	hotel
wa	(subject particle, frequently used in negative sentences)
suki dewa arimasen	don't like
Hoteru wa suki dewa arimasen.	I don't like hotels.
nani	what
o	(direct object particle)

shi-tai	want to do
Nani o shi-tai desu ka?	What do you want to do?
sumō	traditional Japanese wrestling
mi-tai	want to see
Sumō o mi-tai desu.	I want to see sumo.
Fuji-san e	to Mount Fuji
iki-tai	want to go
Fuji-san e iki-tai desu.	I want to go to Mount Fuji.
hanga	woodblock print
kai-tai	want to buy
Hanga o kai-tai desu.	I want to buy woodblock prints.
seto-mono	pottery
yukkuri	slowly
hanashite kudasai	please speak
Yukkuri hanashite kudasai.	Please speak slowly.
shashin	photograph
totte kudasai	please take
Shashin o totte kudasai.	Please take a picture.

Mount Fuji

Japan's most revered mountain, Mount Fuji, is called *Fuji-san* in Japanese. *San*, which here means "mountain" and not "Mr.", is used with other Japanese mountains like Aso-san in Kyushu and Hiei-zan in Kyoto.

At 12,385 feet, Mount Fuji is Japan's highest mountain, and although it last erupted in 1707, it's classified as an active volcano. From the bullet train, you can get a good view of Mount Fuji's superb conical shape. The adventurous can climb it; people of all ages climb Mount Fuji, mostly to see the breathtaking sunrise over the Pacific Ocean.

Expressions in Context

Hanga ga hoshii desu.	I want a woodblock print.
Sumō ga suki desu.	I like sumo.
Hanga wa suki dewa arimasen.	I don't like woodblock prints.
Nani o shi-tai desu ka?	What do you want to do?
Kyōto e iki-tai desu.	I want to go to Kyoto.
Seto-mono o kai-tai desu.	I want to buy some pottery.
Nani o mi-tai desu ka?	What do you want to see?
Fuji-san o mi-tai desu.	I want to see Mount Fuji.
Sumō o mi-tai desu.	I want to see sumo.
Nani o kai-tai desu ka?	What do you want to buy?
Nihon ningyō o kai-tai desu.	I want to buy a Japanese doll.
Sumimasen. Yukkuri hanashite kudasai.	Excuse me. Please speak slowly.
Sumimasen. Shashin o totte kudasai.	Excuse me. Please take my picture.

Additional Words & Expressions

supōtsu	sports
undō	physical exercise
Undō o shi-tai desu.	I'd like to exercise.
umi	ocean
mizuumi	lake
yama	mountain
yama-nobori	mountain climbing
haikingu	hiking
kyanpu	camping
Kyanpu o shi-tai desu.	I want to go camping.
go	board game played with black and white stones
mājan	mahjong
e	painting
chōkoku	sculpture
kottō-hin	antique
Kottō-hin o mi-tai desu.	I want to see some antiques.
Sumimasen. Shashin o totte ii desu ka?	Excuse me. May I take a picture?
Anata no shashin o totte ii desu ka?	May I take your picture?

Shopping

Shop clerks in Japan are polite and eager to help, and if you speak slowly and gesture, you shouldn't have problems making them understand you. Of course, understanding what *they* are saying is a different story. If you're unsure of a price, have a clerk write it down.

Words & Expressions

ikura	how much
Ikura desu ka?	How much is it?
kore	this
Kore wa ikura desu ka?	How much is this?
ni-sen-en	2,000 yen
Ni-sen-en desu.	It's 2,000 yen.
ichi-man-en	10,000 yen
kono tokei	this watch
yon-man san-zen-en	43,000 yen
Kono tokei wa yon-man san-zen-en desu.	This watch is 43,000 yen.
o	(direct object particle)
kudasai	please; please give
Kore o kudasai.	Please give me this. (I'll take this.)

ōkii	big
ōkii-no	big one
misete kudasai	please show
Ōkii-no o misete kudasai.	Please show me a big one.
yasui	inexpensive
yasui-no	inexpensive one
Yasui-no o misete kudasai.	Please show me an inexpensive one.
hoka-no	different one
mō ichido	once more
itte kudasai	please say
Mō ichido itte kudasai.	Please say it once more.
Ei-go de	in English
hanashite kudasai	please speak
Ei-go de hanashite kudasai.	Please speak in English.
Nihon-go de	in Japanese
nedan	price
kaite kudasai	please write
Nedan o kaite kudasai.	Please write down the price.

Folk-Art Handicrafts ─────────

Mingei-hin, colorful folk-art handicrafts, make perfect gifts or souvenirs from Japan. As you travel, keep an eye out for local specialties. Tokyo, for example, is famous for its glass wind chimes *(fūrin),* Kyoto for its folding paper fans *(sensu),* and Tohoku for its delicately hand-painted wooden dolls *(kokeshi).* In most cities, *mingei-hin* are sold at small shops around tourist attractions and train stations. *Mingei* stores in larger cities have wonderful selections and fair prices, but they're often hard to find. It's a good idea to ask for directions.

Expressions in Context

Kore wa ikura desu ka?	How much is this?
Ni-sen-en desu.	It's 2,000 yen.
Ōkii-no wa ikura desu ka?	How much is the big one?
San-zen-en desu.	It's 3,000 yen.
Kono tokei wa ikura desu ka?	How much is this watch?
Yon-man-en desu.	It's 40,000 yen.
Ichi-man-en desu.	It's 10,000 yen.
Kore o kudasai.	Please give me this. (I'll take this.)
Kono tokei o kudasai.	Please give me this watch.
Kono yasui-no o kudasai.	Please give me this inexpensive one.
Kore o misete kudasai.	Please show me this.
Hoka-no o misete kudasai.	Please show me a different one.
Mō ichido misete kudasai.	Please show me once more.
Mō ichido itte kudasai.	Please say it once more.
Nihon-go de hanashite kudasai.	Please speak in Japanese.
Kore o kaite kudasai.	Please write this.

Additional Words & Expressions

USEFUL ADJECTIVES

chiisai	small
takai	expensive
karui	light
omoi	heavy
marui	round
shikakui	square
azayaka	bright
jimi	subdued; refined
hade	flashy; gaudy
utsukushii	beautiful
kirei	pretty
furui	old
atarashii	new
dentō-teki	traditional

JAPANESE PRODUCTS

kinu	silk
ori-mono	cloth; textile
denki-seihin	electrical goods
nuri-mono	lacquerware
seto-mono	pottery
shippō-yaki	cloisonné ware
Imari-yaki	Imari ware
shinju	pearl
sensu	folding fan
mingei-hin	folk-art handicraft
furoshiki	cloth used for wrapping things
tōjiki	chinaware

kake-mono	hanging scroll; hanging picture
kimono	kimono
yukata	light, cotton kimono
chōchin	lantern
washi	traditional, handmade paper
hanga	woodblock print

OTHERS

chotto	a little; a moment
matte kudasai	please wait
Chotto matte kudasai.	Please wait a moment.
okutte kudasai	please send
Kore o okutte kudasai.	Please send this.
tsutsunde kudasai	please wrap
Kore o tsutsunde kudasai.	Please wrap this.

Talking About the Weather

The Japanese believe they discuss the weather more than other people do. True or not, the weather offers you a good way to start a conversation. One thing is certain; the Japanese will be curious to know what type of weather you have in your part of the world.

Words & Expressions

kyō	today
ii	good; nice
tenki	weather
ne	isn't it?
Kyō wa ii tenki desu ne.	It's nice weather today, isn't it?
Sō desu ne.	It is, isn't it?/That's right.
ashita	tomorrow
dō	how
deshō	will be; will probably be
Ashita wa dō deshō ka?	How will the weather be tomorrow?
shūmatsu	weekend
sā	well
ame	rain; rainy

Sā, ame deshō.	Well, it'll probably be rainy.
samui	cold (temperature)
Samui deshō.	It'll probably be cold.
kinō	yesterday
warui tenki	bad weather
deshita	was
Kinō wa warui tenki deshita.	The weather was bad yesterday.
atsui hi	hot day
Atsui hi deshita.	It was a hot day.
Hiroshima	Hiroshima
hare	fine weather
Hiroshima wa hare deshita.	The weather was fine in Hiroshima.
atatakai	warm
Kyō wa atatakai desu ne.	Today is warm, isn't it?
suzushii	cool

Japanese Seasons

Japan has four major seasons—spring, summer, fall, and winter—with rainy periods between spring and summer, and summer and fall. During the fall rainy period, typhoons bring torrential rainfalls to all the country except Hokkaido. Although the part of Japan bordering the Pacific Ocean has little snow in winter, areas like Kanazawa along the Japan Sea have heavy snowfalls that isolate rural villages. The change in landscape is dramatic. From Kyoto, which may have no snow on the ground, a train ride through a series of tunnels will take you to the heart of snow country in a matter of minutes.

Expressions in Context

Kyō wa ii tenki desu ne.	It's nice weather today, isn't it?
Sō desu ne.	It certainly is.
Suzushii desu ne.	Cool, isn't it?
Atsui desu ne.	Hot, isn't it?
Shūmatsu wa dō deshō ka?	How will it be this weekend?
Sā, hare deshō.	Well, it'll probably be fair.
Sā, ii tenki deshō.	Well, it'll probably be nice.
Kinō wa dō deshita ka?	How was yesterday?
Warui tenki deshita.	The weather was bad.
Ame deshita.	It was rainy.
Samui hi deshita.	It was a cold day.
Hiroshima wa dō deshita ka?	How was Hiroshima?
Hare deshita.	The weather was fine.
Ii tenki deshita.	The weather was nice.
Kinō wa warui tenki deshita ka?	Was the weather bad yesterday?
Iie, hare deshita.	No, it was fine.
Atatakai hi deshita.	It was a warm day.

Additional Words & Expressions

kikō	climate
tenki-yohō	weather forecast
Tenki-yohō ni yoru to, ashita wa ame desu.	According to the weather forecast, tomorrow will be rainy.
kishō-dai	weather bureau
ondo	temperature
Kashi	Fahrenheit
do	degree
Kashi nana-jū-do	70 degrees Fahrenheit
Sesshi	Celsius
Sesshi ni-jū-do	20 degrees Celsius
yuki	snow
furimasu	falls (rain, snow)
Ame ga furimasu.	It rains.
kiri	fog
sumoggu	smog
niwaka-ame	shower
kaze	wind
arashi	storm
taifū	typhoon
kaminari	thunder
inazuma	lightning
kumori	cloudy
mushi-atsui	humid
kasa	umbrella

20

Making Reservations

Since making reservations on the phone in Japanese can be very difficult for the foreigner, it's fortunate that many places in Japan employ English-speaking staff to take reservations. Making reservations in person, however, is easier than on the phone. This chapter will teach you what to say.

Words & Expressions

kankō-basu	tour bus
yoyaku	reservation
o-negai shimasu	please
Kankō-basu no yoyaku, o-negai shimasu.	I'd like to make a reservation for the tour bus.
Itsu desu ka?	For when?
Ashita desu.	For tomorrow.
kyō	today
man'in	full; no vacancy
Sumimasen ga, ashita wa man'in desu.	Sorry, but we're full tomorrow.
asatte	the day after tomorrow
dō	how about
Asatte wa dō desu ka?	How about the day after tomorrow?

daijōbu	all right
Asatte wa daijōbu desu.	The day after tomorrow is all right.
jā	well then
Jā, asatte yoyaku, o-negai shimasu.	Well then, please make the reservation for the day after tomorrow.
nan-nin-sama	how many people
-sama	polite equivalent to -*san*
Nan-nin-sama desu ka?	How many people?
futari	two people
Futari desu.	There are two people.
hitori	one person
kippu	ticket
ikura	how much
Kippu wa ikura desu ka?	How much is the ticket?
San-zen go-hyaku-en desu.	It's 3,500 yen.
O-namae wa?	What's your name?
Sumisu desu.	It's Smith.

Unique Accommodations

If you want to experience lodging Japanese style, stay at a Japanese inn *(ryokan)*. You'll be served a complete Japanese dinner and breakfast, and you'll sleep on bedding laid out on *tatami* (straw mat) floors. Or, try a *minshuku,* a family-run guesthouse offering lodging at a reasonable price.

For a unique experience, spend a night at a temple. Besides being able to sample the delicious and healthy temple cooking, you'll get a feel of the serenity and simplicity of temple living. Ask your travel agent or the Japan Travel Bureau for more information.

Expressions in Context

Kankō-basu no yoyaku, o-negai shimasu.	I'd like to make a reservation for the tour bus.
Itsu desu ka?	For when?
Kyō desu.	For today.
Asatte desu.	For the day after tomorrow.
Nan-nin-sama desu ka?	How many people are there?
Hitori desu.	One person.
O-namae wa?	What's your name?
Sumisu desu.	My name is Smith.
Kippu wa ikura desu ka?	How much is the ticket?
San-zen-en desu.	It's 3,000 yen.
Sumimasen ga, kyō wa man'in desu.	Sorry, but we're full for today.
Ashita wa dō desu ka?	How about tomorrow?
Ashita wa daijōbu desu.	Tomorrow is all right.
Jā, ashita, o-negai shimasu.	Well, then please make it for tomorrow.

Additional Words & Expressions

LODGING FACILITIES

furonto	front desk; reception desk
robii	lobby
rōka	hall; corridor
erebētā	elevator
kaidan	stairs
shokudō	dining hall
o-furo	bath (communal bath)

RESERVATIONS AND CHECK-IN

heya	room
rūmu	room
shinguru-rūmu	single room
daburu-rūmu	double room
tsuin	twin room
basu-rūmu	bathroom
basu-tsuki no heya	room with a bathroom
ip-paku	overnight stay
ni-haku	two-night stay
Ni-haku shimasu.	We'll stay two nights.
san-paku	three-night stay
Motto yasui heya ga arimasu ka?	Do you have a cheaper room?
Motto ii heya ga arimasu ka?	Do you have a better room?
kagi	key
kōri	ice
Kōri, kudasai.	May I have some ice please?
san-nin	three people

| yo-nin | four people |
| go-nin | five people |

CHECK-OUT

o-kanjo	bill
ryōkin	charge
muryō	no charge
sābisu-ryō	service charge
zeikin	tax
uketori	receipt

OTHERS

Hachi-ji ni okoshite kudasai.	Please wake me at 8:00.
Kore o yūbin de dashite kudasai.	Please put this in the mail.
Kitte ga arimasu ka?	Do you have stamps?
Sentaku wa o-negai dekimasu ka?	Can I have this laundered?
reibō-sōchi	air conditioner
Reibō-sōchi ga yokunai desu.	The air conditioner does not work very well.
danbō-sōchi	heater
Danbō-sōchi ga yokunai desu.	The heater does not work very well.

Help!

If you need help as you're wandering about on foot, go to a "police box" (*kōban*), usually located near train stations and street corners. Look for a small building with a policeman standing in front. The policemen on duty will gladly assist you in any way, even if it's just helping with directions.

Words & Expressions

Tasukete!	Help!
Tasukete kudasai.	Please help me.
Komatte imasu.	I'm in trouble.
Dō shimashita ka?	What happened?
Byōki desu.	I'm sick.
kippu	ticket
o	(direct object particle)
nakushimashita	lost
Kippu o nakushimashita.	I lost my ticket.
densha ni	on the train
kamera	camera
Densha ni kamera o wasuremashita.	I forgot my camera on the train.
saifu	wallet
michi	way; road

108

ni mayoimashita	lost (the way)
Michi ni mayoimashita.	I lost my way.
hoteru	hotel
wa	(subject particle)
doko	where
wakarimasen	don't know; can't find
Hoteru wa doko ka **wakarimasen.**	I don't know where my hotel is.
koko	here; this place
Koko wa doko desu ka?	Where am I?
denwa	telephone
Denwa wa doko desu ka?	Where's a telephone?
kyūkyū-sha	ambulance
yonde kudasai	please call
Kyūkyū-sha o yonde kudasai.	Please call an ambulance.
Ei-go	English language
hanasu hito	person who speaks
Ei-go o hanasu hito o yonde **kudasai.**	Please call a person who speaks English.

Useful Telephone Numbers

For travel information in English, call the Tourist Information Center (TIC). In Tokyo, their number is (03) 502-1461; in Kyoto, (075) 371-5649; and at Narita Airport, (0476) 32-8711. For tourist information about eastern Japan, dial toll-free 0120-222-800; for western Japan, 0120-444-800. English directory assistance in Tokyo is (03) 201-1010 and (045) 322-1010 in Yokohama.

For the police, dial 110 anywhere in the country. For reporting a fire or calling an ambulance, the number nationwide is 119.

Expressions in Context

Tasukete!	Help!
Komatte imasu.	I'm in trouble.
Tasukete kudasai.	Please help me.
Dō shimashita ka?	What happened?
Byōki desu.	I'm sick.
Kyūkyū-sha o yonde kudasai.	Please call an ambulance.
Komatte imasu. Tasukete kudasai.	I'm in trouble. Please help me.
Dō shimashita ka?	What happened?
Michi ni mayoimashita.	I lost my way.
Hoteru wa doko desu ka?	Where's the hotel?
Denwa wa doko desu ka?	Where's a telephone?
Kippu o nakushimashita.	I lost my ticket.
Kamera o nakushimashita.	I lost my camera.
Densha ni saifu o wasuremashita.	I forgot my wallet on the train.
Wakarimasen.	I don't understand.
Ei-go o hanasu hito o yonde kudasai.	Please call a person who speaks English.

Additional Words & Expressions

HEALTH

isha	doctor
Isha o yonde kudasai.	Please call a doctor.
Ei-go o hanasu isha	English-speaking doctor
kusuri	medicine
byōin	hospital
kango-fu	nurse
chūsha	injection; shot
kega	injury
taion-kei	thermometer
netsu	fever
Netsu ga arimasu.	I have a fever.
itai	hurt
atama	head
Atama ga itai desu.	My head hurts.
o-naka	stomach
ha	tooth
ashi	foot; leg
te	hand
harete imasu	swollen
Ashi ga harete imasu.	My foot is swollen.
mame	blister
Mame ga dekimashita.	I've developed a blister.
geri	diarrhea
Geri o shite imasu.	I've got diarrhea.
kaze	cold
kaze-gusuri	cold medicine
Kaze o hiite imasu.	I have a cold.
Kono kusuri ga arimasu ka?	Do you have this medicine?

Nani-ka arimasu ka?

Do you have (some medicine) for me?

kanpō-yaku

Chinese medicine

OTHERS
o-kane money
pasupōto passport
toraberāzu-chekku traveler's checks
Toraberāzu-chekku o nakushimashita. I lost my traveler's checks.
ryōji-kan consulate
taishi-kan embassy
keisatsu-sho police station
kōban police box
dorobō thief
Dorobō ni nusumaremashita. I was robbed by a thief.

Dictionary

This dictionary has over 1,800 words and expressions needed for daily life in Japan. All entries appearing in the text have been included. Note that Japanese verbs are given in the polite *(-masu)* present form. In the Japanese-English section, the honorific *o* for most nouns has been dropped. If you have difficulty finding a noun in the dictionary, check to see if it begins with *o*. If it does, disregard this *o* and search for the word under its second letter. For example, in the dictionary, *o-hana* (flower) appears as *hana*.

English-Japanese

admission fee	nyūjō-ryō
admission ticket	nyūjō-ken
adult	otona
after ~	ato; ~ no ato
again	mata
air conditioner	reibō-sōchi
airplane	hikō-ki
airport	kūkō
alarm clock	mezamashi-dokei
all right	daijōbu
alone	hitori
a.m.	gozen
ambulance	kyūkyū-sha
America	Amerika
American (person)	Amerika-jin
amusement park	yūen-chi
animal	dōbutsu
anniversary	kinen-bi
antique	kottō(-hin)
apple	ringo
appointment	yakusoku
April	Shi-gatsu
archway (Shinto shrine)	torii
arrival time	tōchaku-jikan
at	de
August	Hachi-gatsu
Australia	Ōsutoraria

Australian (person)	Ōsutoraria-jin
autumn	aki
bad	warui
bag; baggage	nimotsu
baggage checkroom	te-nimotsu ichiji azukari-jo
bakery	pan-ya
bamboo shoot	takenoko
bank	ginkō
banquet	enkai
bar	bā
baseball	yakyū
baseball game	yakyū no shiai
basement	chika
bath	o-furo
bathroom	basu-rūmu; o-tearai
bean paste	miso
beautiful	utsukushii
beef	gyū-niku
beer	biiru
before ~	mae; ~ no mae (ni)
behind ~	ushiro; ~ no ushiro (ni)
beverage	nomi-mono
big	ōkii
bird	tori
birthday	tanjō-bi
bitter	nigai
black tea	kōcha
boarding area; landing	nori-ba
book	hon
bookstore	hon-ya

borrow (verb)	karimasu
please borrow	karite kudasai
botanical garden	shokubutsu-en
bought	kaimashita
bound for ~	-yuki
box lunch	bentō
box lunch (sold at a station)	eki-ben
boy	otoko no ko
breakfast	asa-gohan
break into small money (verb)	kuzushimasu
please break into small money	kuzushite kudasai
break-up; disperse (verb)	kaisan shimasu
break-up time; dispersal time	kaisan-jikan
bright	azayaka
brother (see older brother, younger brother)	
buckwheat noodle	o-soba
Buddha	Hotoke-sama
Buddha (large statue of)	daibutsu
Buddhist temple	o-tera
building	biru
bullet train	Shinkansen
bus	basu
bus stop	basu-teiryūjo; basu-tei
buy (verb)	kaimasu
doesn't buy; don't buy	kaimasen
please buy	katte kudasai
cabbage	kyabetsu
calendar	karendā

call (verb)	yobimasu
please call	yonde kudasai
camera	kamera
camera shop	kamera-ya
camping	kyanpu
can; is able	dekimasu
Canada	Kanada
Canadian (person)	Kanada-jin
can't; isn't able	dekimasen
car	kuruma
carrot	ninjin
castle	shiro
cat	neko
catch a cold (verb)	kaze o hikimasu
Celsius	Sesshi
Certainly, sir/ma'am.	Kashikomarimashita.
charge; fee	ryōkin
check; bill	o-kanjō
checkers (Japanese board game)	go
check-out time	chekku-auto taimu
chicken	tori-niku
child; children	kodomo
China	Chūgoku
chinaware; ceramics	tōjiki
Chinese (language)	Chūgoku-go
Chinese (person)	Chūgoku-jin
Chinese cuisine	Chūgoku-ryōri
chopsticks	o-hashi
church	kyōkai
city; town	machi

country · 119

climate	kikō
clock	tokei
cloisonné	shippō-yaki
closing hour of a store	heiten-jikan
cloth (for wrapping)	furoshiki
cloth; textile	ori-mono
cloudy	kumori
Coca-Cola	Koka-kōra
cocktail party	kakuteru-pātii
coffee	kōhii
coffee shop	kissa-ten
cold (sickness)	kaze
cold (temperature)	samui
cold (to the touch)	tsumetai
cold day	samui hi
cold medicine	kaze-gusuri
college; university	daigaku
come (verb)	kimasu
please come	kite kudasai
company	kaisha
company employee	kaisha-in
concert	konsāto
conductor (train)	shashō
conference; meeting	kaigi
Congratulations!	Omedetō gozaimasu!
consulate	ryōji-kan
cookie	kukkii
cool	suzushii
corn	tōmorokoshi
corner	kado
country; rural area	inaka

crab	kani
credit card	kurejitto-kādo
cucumber	kyūri
cup; glass	koppu
curry with rice	karē-raisu
customer	o-kyaku
daughter (one's own)	musume
daughter (someone else's)	musume-san
day after tomorrow	asatte
day before yesterday	ototoi
day off; holiday	yasumi
December	Jū-ni-gatsu
deer	shika
degree	do
delicious; tasty	oishii
dentist	ha-isha
department store	depāto
departure time	shuppatsu-jikan
diarrhea	geri
did	shimashita
different; another	hoka
different one	hoka-no
dining car	shokudō-sha
dining hall	shokudō
do (verb)	shimasu
doesn't do; don't do	shimasen
please do	shite kudasai
doctor	isha
dog	inu
doll	ningyō

door	doa
double room	daburu-rūmu
down	shita
drink (verb)	nomimasu
please drink	nonde kudasai
drink; beverage	nomi-mono
early	hayaku
east	higashi
eat (verb)	tabemasu
please eat	tabete kudasai
egg	tamago
eggplant	nasu
eight	hachi; yattsu
eighth day of the month	yōka
electrical goods	denki-seihin
elevator	erebētā
embassy	taishi-kan
England	Igirisu
English (language)	Ei-go
English (person)	Igirisu-jin
entrance	iriguchi
escalator	esukarētā
evening	yūgata
everyday	mai-nichi
every night	mai-ban
every week	mai-shū
every year	mai-nen
exchange money (verb)	ryō-gae shimasu
please exchange money	ryō-gae shite kudasai
excursion boat	yūran-sen

Excuse me.	Sumimasen.
exhibition	tenran-kai
exit	deguchi
expensive	takai
exposition	hakuran-kai
express train	kyūkō
expressway	kōsoku-dōro
extension	naisen
Fahrenheit	Kashi
fall (verb, used for rain, snow)	furimasu
it rains	ame ga furimasu
it snows	yuki ga furimasu
famous	yūmei
far	tōi
fare	unchin; ryōkin
fare table/listing	unchin-hyō
farewell party	sōbetsu-kai
father (one's own)	chichi
father (someone else's; and when addressing one's own)	otōsan
February	Ni-gatsu
female	onna; josei
ferry boat	ferii
festival	o-matsuri
fever	netsu
field trip; tour of a factory	kengaku-ryokō
fifth day of the month	itsuka
film	firumu
fine	rippa

fine; healthy	genki
fine weather	hare
fireworks	hanabi
fireworks display	hanabi-taikai
first day of the month	tsuitachi
fish	sakana
five	go; itsutsu
flashy; gaudy	hade
floor	yuka
floor (story)	kai
fog	kiri
folding fan	sensu
folding screen	byōbu
folk-art handicraft	mingei-hin
for; of	no
forget (verb)	wasuremasu
please forget	wasurete kudasai
fork	fōku
four	shi/yon; yottsu
fourth day of the month	yokka
France	Furansu
free; no charge	muryō
French (language)	Furansu-go
French (person)	Furansu-jin
Friday	Kin-yōbi
friend	tomodachi
front desk; reception desk	furonto
fruit	kuda-mono
full	ippai
full; no vacancy	man'in
funeral	o-sōshiki

gallery	garō
game; match; tournament	shiai
garden	niwa
gas station	gasorin-sutando
gate (temple)	sanmon
gaudy; flashy	hade
German (language)	Doitsu-go
German (person)	Doitsu-jin
get up (verb)	okimasu
please get up	okite kudasai
gift shop	gifuto-shoppu
girl	onna no ko
Glad to meet you.	Dōzo yoroshiku.
go (verb)	ikimasu
doesn't go; don't go	ikimasen
please go	itte kudasai
golf	gorufu
golf tournament	gorufu no konpe
good	ii
Good afternoon./Hello.	Konnichiwa.
Goodbye.	Sayōnara.
Good evening.	Konbanwa.
Good morning.	Ohayō gozaimasu.
Good night.	Oyasumi-nasai.
grandchild (one's own)	mago
grandchild (someone else's)	o-mago-san
grape	budō
green light	ao-shingō
green tea	o-cha
group tour	dantai-ryokō

guesthouse; inn (family-run)	minshuku
guidebook	gaido-bukku
half	han
hall; corridor	rōka
hand	te
hard; tough	katai
have (verb)	arimasu
he	kare
head	atama
healthy; fine	genki
hear (be able to)	kikoemasu
hear; listen (verb)	kikimasu
please hear	kiite kudasai
heater	danbō-sōchi
heavy	omoi
Hello. (on the telephone)	Moshi-moshi.
Hello. / Good afternoon.	Konnichiwa.
help (verb)	tasukemasu
please help	tasukete kudasai
here; this place	koko
hiking	haikingu
historical site	shiseki
hobby	shumi
holiday; day-off	yasumi
holiday (national)	saijitsu
hospital	byōin
hot	atsui
hot day	atsui hi
hotel	hoteru
hot spring	onsen

how about	ikaga
How are you?/Are you well?	O-genki desu ka?
How do you do?	Hajimemashite.
how; in what way	dōshite
how many	ikutsu
how much	ikura
humid	mushi-atsui
hungry (to be)	o-naka ga suite imasu
hurt	itai
I	watashi
ice	kōri
ice cream	aisu-kuriimu
Imari ware	Imari-yaki
Imperial Hotel	Teikoku Hoteru
Imperial Palace	Kōkyo
in; at	de
in; inside	naka
Indonesia	Indoneshia
Indonesian (language)	Indoneshia-go
Indonesian (person)	Indoneshia-jin
in English	Ei-go de
inexpensive	yasui
information office	annai-jo
injection; shot	chūsha
injury	kega
Inland Sea	Seto-naikai
inn; guesthouse	minshuku
inn (traditional)	ryokan
international telephone call	kokusai-denwa
intersection	kōsaten

is; am; are	desu
isn't; am not; aren't	dewa arimasen
isn't it?/aren't you?	ne
Italian (language)	Itaria-go
Italian (person)	Itaria-jin
Italy	Itaria
January	Ichi-gatsu
Japanese (language)	Nihon-go
Japanese (person)	Nihon-jin
Japanese cuisine	Nihon-ryōri
Japanese inn	ryokan
Japanese wrestling	sumō
July	Shichi-gatsu
June	Roku-gatsu
Kabuki	kabuki
Kabuki Theater	Kabuki-za
key	kagi
kimono	kimono
kimono (light, cotton)	yukata
kiosk; station shop	kiosuku; eki no baiten
Korea (ROK)	Kankoku
Korean (language)	Kankoku-go
Korean (person)	Kankoku-jin
lacquerware	nuri-mono
lake	mizuumi
lantern	chōchin
last month	sengetsu
last week	senshū

last year	kyonen
late	osoi
laundry	sentaku-mono
lawyer	bengo-shi
leave; go out (verb)	dekakemasu; demasu
please leave	dete kudasai
left	hidari
leg	ashi
lend (verb)	kashimasu
please lend	kashite kudasai
let off (verb)	oroshimasu
please let (me) off	oroshite kudasai
letter	tegami
lettuce	retasu
library	tosho-kan
light	karui
lightning	inazuma
like; be fond of	suki
limited-express ticket	tokkyū-ken
limited-express train	tokkyū
line (train)	sen
listen (verb)	kikimasu
please listen	kiite kudasai
lobby	robii
local telephone call	shinai-denwa
local train	futsū
long-distance telephone call	chōkyori-denwa
look (verb)	mimasu
please look	mite kudasai
looked	mimashita
lose (verb)	nakushimasu

lose the way (verb)	michi ni mayoimasu
lotus root	renkon
lunch	hiru-gohan
magazine	zasshi
mahjong	mājan
mail (a letter)	yūbin de dashimasu
please mail	yūbin de dashite kudasai
male	otoko
man	otoko no hito
many; much	takusan
map	chizu
March	San-gatsu
May	Go-gatsu
meal	gohan; shokuji
meal (meal included)	shokuji-tsuki
meat	niku
medicine	kusuri
meeting; conference	kaigi
meeting time	shūgō-jikan
melon	meron
message	messēji
milk	gyūnyū
minute (suffix used for)	-fun
moment; awhile	shibaraku
Monday	Getsu-yōbi
money	o-kane
monorail	monorēru
monument	kinen-hi
moon viewing	tsuki-mi

more	motto
morning	asa
mother (one's own)	haha
mother (someone else's; and when addressing one's own)	okāsan
mountain	yama
mountain climbing	yama-nobori
Mount Fuji	Fuji-san
movie	eiga
movie theater	eiga-kan
Mr. / Mrs. / Ms. / Miss	-san
museum	hakubutsu-kan
mushroom	shiitake
name	namae
napkin	napukin
national holiday	saijitsu
near	chikai
nearby	soba
new; fresh	atarashii
newspaper	shinbun
next month	raigetsu
next week	raishū
next year	rainen
night	yoru
nine	kyū/ku; kokonotsu
ninth day of the month	kokonoka
no	iie
No, thank you.	Kekkō desu.
nonsmoking car	kin'en-sha

noodle (dark and thin)	soba
noodle (white and fat)	udon
noon	hiru
north	kita
November	Jū-ichi-gatsu
now	ima
nurse	kango-fu
occupation; work	shigoto
ocean	umi
o'clock (suffix used for)	-ji
October	Jū-gatsu
octopus	tako
of; for	no
old (not young)	toshi-totta
old; stale	furui
older brother (one's own)	ani
older brother (someone else's; and when addressing one's own)	oniisan
older sister (one's own)	ane
older sister (someone else's; and when addressing one's own)	onēsan
once more	mō ichido
one	ichi; hitotsu
one hundred	hyaku
one person	hitori
one thousand	sen
one-thousand yen note	sen-en-satsu
one-way (ticket)	katamichi(-kippu)

onion	tamanegi
opening hour of a store	kaiten-jikan
orange	orenji
orange juice	orenji-jūsu
out; outside	soto
overnight stay	ip-paku
over there	asoko
oyster bed	kaki-yōshokujo
Pacific Ocean	Taihei-yō
pagoda; tower	tō
painting	e
paper	kami
paper (traditional, hand-made)	washi
park	kōen
parking lot	chūsha-jō
party	pātii
passport	pasupōto
peace	heiwa
peach	momo
pearl	shinju
persimmon	kaki
person	hito
pharmacy	kusuri-ya; yakkyoku
photo	shashin
physical exercise	undō
pickle	tsuke-mono
picnic	pikunikku
picture	e
place of interest	meisho

plain; open field	heiya
plate	sara
platform	hōmu
please	dozō; kudasai; o-negai shimasu
p.m.	gogo
police	keisatsu
police box	kōban
police station	keisatsu-sho
poor; unskillful	heta
pork	buta-niku
pork cutlet	ton-katsu
Portugal	Porutogaru
Portuguese (language)	Porutogaru-go
Portuguese (person)	Porutogaru-jin
postcard	e-hagaki; hagaki
post office	yūbin-kyoku
potato	jagaimo
pottery	seto-mono
prefecture	ken
pretty	kirei
previous day	mae no hi
price	nedan
promise; appointment	yakusoku
public square	hiro-ba
public telephone	kōshū-denwa
pumpkin	kabocha
quickly	hayaku
radio	rajio

rain	ame
raw	nama
read (verb)	yomimasu
please read	yonde kudasai
receipt	uketori; ryōshū-sho
reception desk	uketsuke; furonto
redcap; porter	akabō
regional specialty	meisan
reporter; journalist	kisha
reservation	yoyaku
reserved-seat ticket	zaseki shitei-ken
restaurant	resutoran
restroom	o-tearai
return an object (verb)	kaeshimasu
please return	kaeshite kudasai
return home (verb)	kaerimasu
please return home	kaette kudasai
rice	kome; gohan; raisu
rice (cooked)	gohan; raisu
rice bowl	chawan
rice cracker	senbei
rice paddy	suiden
right	migi
right away	sugu
river	kawa
road	michi; dōro
robbed (to be)	nusumaremasu
roof	okujō
room	heya; rūmu
room with a bath	basu-tsuki no heya
round	marui

round-trip (ticket)	ōfuku(-kippu)
Russia	Soren; Roshia
Russian (language)	Roshia-go
Russian (person)	Roshia-jin
saké	o-sake
saké cup	sakazuki
salad	sarada
salty	shoppai
Saturday	Do-yōbi
saw	mimashita
say (verb)	iimasu
please say	itte kudasai
scroll (hanging)	kake-mono
sculpture	chōkoku
season	kisetsu
seaweed	nori
second day of the month	futsuka
secretary	hisho
see (verb)	mimasu
doesn't see; don't see	mimasen
please see	mite kudasai
See you later.	Jā mata.
send (verb)	okurimasu
please send	okutte kudasai
separately	betsu-betsu ni
September	Ku-gatsu
service charge	sābisu-ryō
set meal	teishoku
seven	shichi/nana; nanatsu
seventh day of the month	nanoka

she	kanojo
Shinto shrine	jinja
ship	fune
show (verb)	misemasu
please show	misete kudasai
shower (bath)	shawā
shower (rain)	niwaka-ame
shrimp	ebi
sickness	byōki
sightseeing	kankō
sightseeing bus	kankō-basu
signal	shingō
silk	kinu
single room	shinguru-rūmu
sister (see older sister, younger sister)	
six	roku; muttsu
sixth day of the month	muika
skyscraper	kōsō-biru
sleep; go to bed (verb)	nemasu
please sleep/go to bed	nete kudasai
slowly	yukkuri
small	chiisai
smog	sumoggu
snow	yuki
so	sō
soft; tender	yawarakai
son (one's own)	musuko
son (someone else's)	musuko-san
soon; shortly	mō sugu
Sorry, but...	Sumimasen ga...

soup (Japanese)	sui-mono
soup (Western)	sūpu
south	minami
South Korea	Kankoku
souvenir	o-miyage
Spain	Supein
Spanish (language)	Supein-go
Spanish (person)	Supein-jin
speak (verb)	hanashimasu
please speak	hanashite kudasai
spicy	karai
spoon	supūn
sport	supōtsu
spring (season)	haru
square	shikakui
stadium	sutajiamu
stairs	kaidan
stamp (postal)	kitte
start (verb)	hajimarimasu; hajimemasu
please start	hajimete kudasai
station	eki
station employee	eki-in
station shop	kiosuku; eki no baiten
statue	zō
statue of Buddha	butsuzō
steak	sutēki
steal (verb)	nusumimasu
stomach	o-naka
stop (a car)	tomarimasu; tomemasu
please stop	tomete kudasai
store	mise

storm	arashi
student	gakusei
subway	chika-tetsu
subway station	chika-tetsu no eki
sukiyaki	suki-yaki
summer	natsu
summer vacation	natsu-yasumi
sumo	sumō
Sunday	Nichi-yōbi
supper	ban-gohan
sushi	o-sushi
swell (verb)	haremasu
take (verb)	torimasu
please take	totte kudasai
take a photo	shashin o torimasu
tangerine	mikan
taste	aji
tasty; delicious	oishii
tasty (not); unappetizing	mazui
tax	zeikin
taxi	takushii
taxi stand	takushii-noriba
tea (black)	kōcha
tea (green)	o-cha
teach (verb)	oshiemasu
please teach	oshiete kudasai
teacher	sensei
teacup	yu-nomi
tea field	cha-batake
teatime	o-cha no jikan

telephone	denwa
telephone (verb)	denwa shimasu
please telephone	denwa shite kudasai
telephone book	denwa-chō
telephone card	terefon-kādo
telephone charge/bill	denwa-ryō
telephone number	denwa-bangō
telephone operator	kōkan-shu
television	terebi
temperature	ondo
temple	o-tera
tempura	tenpura
ten	jū; tō
tenth day of the month	tōka
ten thousand	ichi-man
Thai (language)	Tai-go
Thai (person)	Tai-jin
Thailand	Tai
Thank you.	Arigatō./Dōmo arigatō.
Thank you. (I'll have some.)	Itadakimasu.
Thank you. (It was delicious.)	Gochisō-sama deshita.
that	sono; ano
that (pronoun)	sore; are
theater	geki-jō
there is/are; (for animate objects)	imasu
there is/are; have (for inanimate objects)	arimasu
thermometer	taion-kei
thief	dorobō

third day of the month	mikka
this	kono
this (pronoun)	kore
this month	kongetsu
this week	konshū
this year	kotoshi
three	san; mittsu
thunder	kaminari
Thursday	Moku-yōbi
ticket	kippu
ticket machine	(kippu no) jidō-hanbaiki
time a performance starts	kaimaku-jikan
tip	chippu
to	e
to; as far as	made
today	kyō
tofu	tōfu
Tokyo Station	Tōkyō Eki
Tokyo Tower	Tōkyō Tawā
tomato	tomato
tomorrow	ashita
tomorrow morning	ashita no asa
tonight; this evening	kon-ban
tooth	ha
tour	tsuā
tour (of a city)	shinai-kankō
tourist	kankō-kyaku
towel (bath towel)	basu-taoru
towel (hot or cold hand towel)	o-shibori
town; city	machi

track number ~	~ -ban-sen
traditional	dentō-teki
train	densha; ressha
transfer	nori-kae
travel	ryokō
travel (verb)	ryokō shimasu
travel bureau	ryokō-sentā
traveler	ryokō-sha
traveler's check	toraberāzu-chekku
travel insurance	ryokō-hoken
trouble (I'm in trouble.)	komatte imasu
trunk (of a car)	toranku
Tuesday	Ka-yōbi
tuna	maguro
turn (verb)	magarimasu; magemasu
please turn	magatte kudasai
twin room	tsuin
two	ni; futatsu
two people	futari
typhoon	taifū
Ueno Park	Ueno Kōen
umbrella	kasa
unappetizing	mazui
understand (verb)	wakarimasu
doesn't/don't understand	wakarimasen
United States	Amerika
university; college	daigaku
up	ue
vegetable	yasai

vending machine	jidō-hanbaiki
vicinity	hen
Vietnam	Betonamu
Vietnamese (language)	Betonamu-go
Vietnamese (person)	Betonamu-jin
wait (verb)	machimasu
please wait	matte kudasai
waiting room	machiai-shitsu
wake someone up (verb)	okoshimasu
please wake me up	okoshite kudasai
wake up	okimasu
please wake up	okite kudasai
walk (a stroll)	sanpo
walk (verb)	arukimasu
please walk	aruite kudasai
wallet	saifu
want	hoshii
want to buy	kai-tai desu
want to do	shi-tai desu
want to drink	nomi-tai desu
want to eat	tabe-tai desu
want to go	iki-tai desu
want to see	mi-tai desu
war	sensō
warm	atatakai
was	deshita
wash (verb)	araimasu
please wash	aratte kudasai
wash clothes (verb)	sentaku shimasu
please wash clothes	sentaku shite kudasai

watch; clock	tokei
watch; see	mimasu
please watch	mite kudasai
watch shop	tokei-ya
water	mizu
watermelon	suika
weather	tenki
weather bureau	kishō-dai
weather forecast	tenki-yohō
wedding ceremony	kekkon-shiki
Wednesday	Sui-yōbi
weekday	heijitsu
weekend	shūmatsu
welcome party	kangei-kai
well; nicely	yoku
well...	sā...
went	ikimashita
west	nishi
Western cuisine	Seiyō-ryōri
West Germany	Nishi Doitsu
what	nan(i)
what (with what)	nan de
what day of the month	nan-nichi
what day of the week	nan-yōbi
what month	nan-gatsu
what time	nan-ji
what year	nan-nen
when	itsu
where	doko
which	dore
whiskey	uisukii

whiskey and water	mizu-wari
who	dare; dochira-sama
wicket	kaisatsu-guchi
will be; would be; will probably be	deshō
wind	kaze
wind chime	fūrin
window	mado
wine	wain
winter	fuyu
winter vacation	fuyu-yasumi
with what	nan de
woman	onna no hito
wonderful	subarashii
woodblock print	hanga
work; occupation	shigoto
work (verb)	hatarakimasu
wrap (verb)	tsutsumimasu
please wrap	tsutsunde kudasai
write (verb)	kakimasu
please write	kaite kudasai
writer	sakka
wrong	chigaimasu
wrong number	bangō-chigai
year after next	sarai-nen
year before last	ototoshi
yes	hai
yesterday	kinō
yogurt	yōguruto
you	anata

You're welcome.	Dō-itashimashite.
younger brother (one's own)	otōto
younger brother (someone else's)	otōto-san
younger sister (one's own)	imōto
younger sister (someone else's)	imōto-san
your	anata no
zoo	dōbutsu-en

Japanese-English

aisu-kuriimu	ice cream
aji	taste
akabō	redcap; porter
aka-shingō	red light
akemasu	open (verb)
aki	autumn
amai	sweet
ame	rain
Amerika-jin	American (person)
anata	you
anata no	your
ane	older sister (one's own)
ani	older brother (one's own)
annai-jo	information office
ano	that
ao-shingō	green light
araimasu	wash (verb)
arashi	storm
are	that (pronoun)
arigatō	thank you
arimasen	there isn't/aren't (for inanimate objects)
arimasu	there is/are (for inanimate objects)
arukimashita	walked
arukimasu	walk (verb)
asa	morning

asa-gohan	breakfast
asatte	day after tomorrow
ashi	foot; leg
ashita no asa	tomorrow morning
ashita no gogo	tomorrow afternoon
asoko	over there
atama	head
atarashii	new; fresh
atatakai	warm
atsui	hot
atsui hi	hot day
azayaka	bright
bā	bar
bangō-chigai	wrong number
ban-gohan	supper
~-ban-sen	track number ~
basu	bus
basu-rūmu	bathroom; restroom
basu-taoru	bath towel
basu-tei	bus stop
basu-tsuki no heya	room with a bath
bengo-shi	lawyer
Betonamu	Vietnam
Betonamu-go	Vietnamese (language)
Betonamu-jin	Vietnamese (person)
betsu-betsu	separately
biiru	beer
biru	building
bonsai	miniature potted tree or shrub

budō	grape
buta-niku	pork
butsuzō	statue of Buddha
buzā	buzzer
byōbu	folding screen
byōin	hospital
byōki	sickness
cha	green tea
cha-batake	tea field
chawan	rice bowl
chekku-auto taimu	check-out time
chichi	father (one's own)
chigaimasu	wrong
chiisai	small
chika	basement
chikai	near
chikai uchi ni	one of these days
chika-tetsu	subway
chika-tetsu no eki	subway station
chippu	tip
chizu	map
chōchin	lantern
chōkoku	sculpture
chōkyori-denwa	long-distance telephone call
chotto	just a little; just a moment
Chūgoku	China
Chūgoku-go	Chinese (language)
Chūgoku-jin	Chinese (person)
Chūgoku-ryōri	Chinese cuisine

chūsha	injection; shot
chūsha-jō	parking lot
daburu-rūmu	double room
daibutsu	large statue of Buddha
daigaku	college; university
daijōbu	all right
danbō-sōchi	heater
dantai-ryokō	group tour
dare	who
de	at; in; with
deguchi	exit
dekakemasu	leave; go out (verb)
dekimasen	can't; isn't able
dekimasu	can; is able
demasu	leave; go out (verb)
denki-seihin	electrical goods
densha	train
dentō-teki	traditional
denwa	telephone
denwa-bangō	telephone number
denwa-chō	telephone book
denwa-ryō	telephone charge/bill
denwa shimasu	telephone (verb)
depāto	department store
deshita	was; were
deshō	will be; would be; will probably be
desu	is; am; are
dewa arimasen	isn't; am not; aren't
do	degree

dō	how
doa	door
dōbutsu	animal
dōbutsu-en	zoo
dochira-sama	who (polite)
Dō-itashimashite.	You're welcome.
Doitsu-go	German (language)
Doitsu-jin	German (person)
doko	where
dōmo	thanks
dōmo arigatō	thank you
donna	what kind of
dore	which
dōro	road
dorobō	thief
dōshite	how
Do-yōbi	Saturday
dōzo	please
Dōzo yoroshiku.	Glad to meet you.
e	picture
e	to
ebi	shrimp
e-hagaki	postcard
eiga	movie
eiga-kan	movie theater
Ei-go	English (language)
Ei-go de	in English
eki	station
eki-ben	box lunch sold at stations
eki-in	station employee

eki no baiten	station shop
enkai	banquet
erebētā	elevator
esukarētā	escalator
ferii	ferryboat
firumu	film (roll of)
fōku	fork
Fuji-san	Mount Fuji
-fun	minute (suffix used for)
fune	ship
Furansu	France
Furansu-go	French (language)
Furansu-jin	French (person)
~~furimasu~~	fall (verb, used for rain, snow)
fūrin	wind chime
furo	bath
furonto	front desk; reception desk
furoshiki	cloth used for wrapping things
furui	old; stale
fusuma	sliding screen
futari	two people
futatsu	two (objects)
futsū	local train
futsū	ordinary
futsuka	second day of the month
fuyu	winter
fuyu-yasumi	winter vacation

ga	(subject particle)
gaido-bukku	guidebook
gakusei	student
garō	gallery
gasorin-sutando	gas station
geki-jō	theater
genki	healthy; fine
geri	diarrhea
Getsu-yōbi	Monday
gifuto-shoppu	gift shop
ginkō	bank
Ginza	(place name in Tokyo)
go	five
go	Japanese board game
Gochisō-sama deshita.	Thank you. (It was delicious.)
Go-gatsu	May
gogo	p.m.
gohan	meal; cooked rice
gorufu	golf
-gō-sha	car # ~
gozen	a.m.
gyū-niku	beef
gyū-nyū	milk
ha	tooth
hachi	eight
Hachi-gatsu	August
hade	flashy; gaudy
hagaki	postcard

haha	mother (one's own)
hai	yes
haikingu	hiking
ha-isha	dentist
hajimarimasu	start (verb)
Hajimemashite.	How do you do?
hajimemasu	start (verb)
hakubutsu-kan	museum
hakuran-kai	exposition
han	half
hanabi	fireworks
hanabi-taikai	fireworks display
hanashimasu	speak (verb)
hanga	woodblock print
hare	fine weather
haremasu	swell (verb)
haru	spring (season)
hashi	chopsticks
hatarakimasu	work (verb)
hayaku	early; quickly
heijitsu	weekday
heiten-jikan	hour a store closes
heiwa	peace
heiya	plain; open field
hen	vicinity
heta	poor; unskillful
heya	room
hidari	left
higashi	east
hikimasu	catch (a cold); pull (verb)
hikō-ki	airplane

hiro-ba	public square
hiru	noon
hiru-gohan	lunch
hisho	secretary
hito	person
hitori	one person; alone
hitotsu	one (object)
hoka-no	different one
hōmu	platform
hon	book
hon-ya	bookstore
hoshii	want
hoteru	hotel
Hotoke-sama	Buddha
hyaku	hundred
ichi	one
Ichi-gatsu	January
ichi-man	ten thousand
Igirisu	England
Igirisu-jin	English (person)
ii	good
iie	no
iimasu	say (verb)
ika	cuttlefish
ikaga	how about
ikimasen	doesn't go; don't go
ikimashita	went
ikimasu	go (verb)
ikura	how much
ikutsu	how many

ima	now
Imari-yaki	Imari ware
imasen	there isn't/aren't (for animate objects)
imasu	there is/are (for animate objects)
imōto	younger sister (one's own)
imōto-san	younger sister (someone else's)
inaka	country; rural area
inazuma	lightning
Indoneshia	Indonesia
Indoneshia-go	Indonesian (language)
Indoneshia-jin	Indonesian (person)
inu	dog
ippai	full; no vacancy
ip-paku	overnight stay
iriguchi	entrance
isha	doctor
Itadakimasu.	Thank you. (I'll have some.)
itai	hurt
Itaria	Italy
Itaria-go	Italian (language)
Itaria-jin	Italian (person)
itsu	when
itsuka	fifth day of the month
itsutsu	five (objects)
itte kudasai	please say
jagaimo	potato

Jā mata.	See you later.
-ji	o'clock / hours (suffix for)
jidō-hanbaiki	vending machine
jikoku-hyo	timetable
jimi	subdued; refined
jinja	Shinto shrine
jiyū-seki	nonreserved seat
jū	ten
jūdō	Japanese art of self-defense
Jū-gatsu	October
Jū-ichi-gatsu	November
Jū-ni-gatsu	December
ka	(question particle)
kabocha	pumpkin
kabuki	Kabuki; Kabuki performance
Kabuki-za	Kabuki Theater
kado	corner
kaerimasu	return home (verb)
kaeshimasu	return an object (verb)
kagi	key
kai	floor (story)
kaidan	stairs
kaigai ryokō	overseas travel
kaigi	meeting; conference
kaimaku-jikan	time a performance starts
kaimasen	doesn't buy; don't buy
kaimashita	bought
kaimasu	buy (verb)
kaisan-jikan	break-up time

kaisan shimasu	breakup; disperse (verb)
kaisatsu-guchi	wicket
kaisha-in	company employee
kaiten-jikan	opening hour of a store
kake-mono	hanging scroll
kaki	persimmon
kakimasu	write (verb)
kaki-yōshokujō	oyster bed
kakuteru-pātii	cocktail party
kamera	camera
kamera-ya	camera shop
kami	paper
kaminari	thunder
Kanada	Canada
Kanada-jin	Canadian (person)
Kanda	(place name in Tokyo)
kane	money
kangei-kai	welcome party
kango-fu	nurse
kani	crab
kanjō	check; bill
kankō	sightseeing
kankō-basu	sightseeing bus
Kankoku	Korea (ROK)
Kankoku-go	Korean (language)
Kankoku-jin	Korean (person)
kankō-kyaku	tourist
kanojo	she
kanpō-yaku	Chinese medicine
karai	spicy
karendā	calendar

karē-raisu	curry with rice
karimasu	borrow (verb)
karui	light
kasa	umbrella
kashi	sweets
Kashi	Fahrenheit
Kashikomarimashita.	Certainly, sir/ma'am.
kashimasu	lend (verb)
kashite kudasai	please lend it
katai	hard; tough
katamichi(-kippu)	one-way (ticket)
kawa	river
Ka-yōbi	Tuesday
kaze	cold (sickness)
kaze	wind
kaze-gusuri	cold medicine
kaze o hikimasu	catch a cold (verb)
kega	injury
keisatsu	police
keisatsu-sho	police station
kēki	cake
Kekkō desu.	No, thank you.
kekkon-shiki	wedding ceremony
ken	prefecture
kenbutsu	sightseeing
kengaku-ryokō	field trip; tour of a factory, institution, etc.
kikimasu	hear; listen (verb)
kikō	climate
kikoemasu	can hear
kimono	kimono; Japanese clothes

kinen-bi	anniversary
kinen-hi	monument
kin'en-sha	nonsmoking car
kinō	yesterday
kinu	silk
Kin-yōbi	Friday
kiosuku	kiosk; station shop
kippu	ticket
kirei	pretty
kiri	fog
kisetsu	season
kisha	reporter; journalist
kishō-dai	weather bureau
kissa-ten	coffee shop
kita	north
kitte	stamp
kōban	police box
kōcha	black tea
kodomo	child; children
kōen	park
kōhii	coffee
Koka-kōra	Coca-Cola
kōkan-shu	telephone operator
koko	here; this place
kokonoka	ninth day of the month
kokonotsu	nine (objects)
kokusai-denwa	international telephone call
Kōkyo	Imperial Palace
Komatte imasu.	I'm in trouble.
kome	rice
konban	tonight; this evening

Konbanwa.	Good evening.
kongetsu	this month
Konnichiwa.	Hello./Good afternoon.
kono	this
konsāto	concert
konshū	this week
koppu	cup; glass
kore	this (pronoun)
korekuto-kōru	collect call
kōri	ice
kōsaten	intersection
kōshū-denwa	public phone
kōsō-biru	skyscraper
kōsoku-dōro	expressway
kotoshi	this year
kottō(-hin)	antique
ku	nine
kuda-mono	fruit
kudasai	please; please give me
Ku-gatsu	September
kukkii	cookie
kūkō	airport
kumori	cloudy
kurejitto-kādo	credit card
kuruma	car
kusuri	medicine
kusuri-ya	pharmacy
kuzushimasu	break into small money (verb)
kyabetsu	cabbage
kyaku	customer

kyanpu	camping
kyō	today
kyōkai	church
kyonen	last year
kyū	nine
kyūka	day off
kyūkō	express train
kyūkyū-sha	ambulance
kyūri	cucumber
machi	town; city
machiai-shitsu	waiting room
machimasu	wait (verb)
made	to; as far as
mado	window
mae	before
mae no hi	previous day
magarimasu	turn (verb)
mago	grandchild (one's own)
maguro	tuna
mai-ban	every night
mai-getsu	every month
mai-nen	every year
mai-nichi	everyday
mai-shū	every week
mājan	mahjong
mame	blister
man'in	full; no vacancy
manjū	bun with bean-jam filling
marui	round
mata	again

matsuri	festival
mayoimasu	lose the way
mazui	not tasty
meisan	regional specialty
meisho	place of interest; tourist spot
meron	melon
messēji	message
mezamashi-dokei	alarm clock
michi	way; road
migi	right
mikan	tangerine
mikka	third day of the month
mimasen	doesn't see; don't see
mimashita	saw
mimasu	see; look; watch (verb)
minami	south
mingei-hin	folk-art handicraft
minshuku	family-run guesthouse/inn
mise	store
misemasu	show (verb)
miso	bean paste
mittsu	three (objects)
miyage	souvenir
mizu	water
mizuumi	lake
mizu-wari	whiskey and water
mō ichido	once more
Moku-yōbi	Thursday
momo	peach
monorēru	monorail

Moshi-moshi.	Hello. (on the telephone)
mō sugu	soon; shortly
motto	more; some more
muika	sixth day of the month
muryō	no charge
mushi-atsui	humid
musuko	son (one's own son)
musuko-san	son (someone else's)
musume	daughter (one's own)
musume-san	daughter (someone else's)
muttsu	six (objects)
naisen	extension
naka	in; inside
nakushimasu	lose (verb)
nama	raw
namae	name
nan(i)	what
nana	seven
nanatsu	seven (objects)
nan de	with what
nan-gatsu	what month
nan-ji	what time
nan-nen	what year
nanoka	the seventh
napukin	napkin
nashi	pear
nasu	eggplant
natsu	summer
natsu-yasumi	summer vacation
ne	isn't it?/aren't you?

nedan	price
neko	cat
nemasu	go to bed; sleep (verb)
netsu	fever
ni	at; in; on
ni	two
Nichi-yōbi	Sunday
nigai	bitter
Ni-gatsu	February
nigiri-zushi, ichinin-mae	set order of sushi for one person
Nihon-go	Japanese (language)
Nihon-jin	Japanese (person)
Nihon-ryōri	Japanese cuisine
Nikkō	(place name)
niku	meat
nimotsu	bag; baggage
ningyō	doll
ninjin	carrot
nishi	west
nishoku-tsuki	two meals included
niwa	garden
niwaka-ame	shower (rain)
no	of; for
~ no ato (de)	after ~
~ no mae (ni)	before ~
nomimasu	drink (verb)
nomi-mono	drink; beverage
nori	seaweed
nori-ba	boarding area; landing
nori-kae	transfer

nuri-mono	lacquerware
nusumimasu	steal (verb)
nyūjō-ken	admission ticket
nyūjō-ryō	admission fee
o	(direct object particle)
o-	(honorific prefix)
o-cha no jikan	teatime
ōfuku(-kippu)	round-trip (ticket)
O-genki desu ka?	How are you?/Are you well?
Ohayō gozaimasu.	Good morning.
oishii	delicious
okāsan	mother (someone else's; and when addressing one's own)
ōkii	big
ōkii-no	big one
okimasu	get up (verb)
okoshimasu	wake someone up (verb)
okujō	roof
okurimasu	send (verb)
o-machi kudasai	please wait
o-mago-san	grandchild (someone else's)
Omedetō gozaimasu!	Congratulations!
omoi	heavy
o-naka	stomach
O-naka ga suite imasu.	I'm hungry.
O-namae wa?	What's your name?
ondo	temperature
o-negai shimasu	please

onēsan	older sister (someone else's; and when addressing one's own)
oniisan	older brother (someone else's; and when addressing one's own)
onna	female
onna no hito	woman
onna no ko	girl
onsen	hot spring
orenji	orange
orenji-jūsu	orange juice
ori-mono	cloth; textile
oroshimasu	let off (verb)
o-shibori	hot or cold hand towel used for wiping one's hands
oshiemasu	teach; tell (verb)
osoku	late
Ōsutoraria	Australia
Ōsutoraria-jin	Australian (person)
o-tearai	restroom; bathroom
otoko	male
otoko no hito	man
otoko no ko	boy
otona	adult
otōsan	father (someone else's; and when addressing one's own)
otōto	younger brother (one's own)

ototoi	day before yesterday
otōto-san	younger brother (someone else's)
ototoshi	year before last
Oyasumi-nasai.	Good night.
pan-ya	bakery
pasupōto	passport
pātii	party
pikunikku	picnic
Porutogaru	Portugal
Porutogaru-go	Portuguese (language)
Porutogaru-jin	Portuguese (person)
raigetsu	next month
rainen	next year
raishū	next week
raisu	rice
rajio	radio
reibō-sōchi	air conditioner
renkon	lotus root
ressha	train
resutoran	restaurant
retasu	lettuce
ringo	apple
rippa	fine
robii	lobby
rōka	hall; corridor
rokkā	locker
roku	six
Roku-gatsu	June

Roshia	Russia
Roshia-go	Russian (language)
Roshia-jin	Russian (person)
rūmu	room
ryō-gae shimasu	exchange money (verb)
ryōji-kan	consulate
ryokan	inn (traditional)
ryōkin	fare
ryokō	travel; trip
ryokō-hoken	travel insurance
ryokō-sentā	travel bureau
ryokō-sha	traveler
ryokō shimasu	travel (verb)
ryōshū-sho	receipt
sā	well
sābisu-ryō	service charge
saifu	wallet
saijitsu	national holiday
sakana	fish
sakazuki	saké cup
sake	alcohol; Japanese alcoholic beverage
sakka	writer
samui	cold (temperature)
samui hi	cold day
san	three
-san	Mr. / Mrs. / Ms. / Miss
San-gatsu	March
sanmon	temple gate
sanpo	walk

sara	plate
sarada	salad
sarai-nen	year after next
sashimi	sliced raw fish
Sayōnara.	Goodbye.
Seiyō-ryōri	Western cuisine
sen	one thousand
-sen	line (train)
senbei	rice cracker
sen-en-satsu	1,000-yen note
sengetsu	last month
sensei	teacher
sen-senshū	week before last
senshū	last week
sensō	war
sensu	folding fan
sentaku suru	wash clothes (verb)
Sesshi	Celsius
seto-mono	pottery
Seto-naikai	Inland Sea
shashin	photo
shashō	conductor (train)
shawā ʹ	shower
shi	four
shiai	game; match; tournament
shibaraku	moment; awhile
shichi	seven
Shichi-gatsu	July
Shi-gatsu	April
shigoto	occupation; work
shiitake	type of mushroom

shika	deer
shikakui	square
shimasen	doesn't do; don't do
shimashita	did
shimasu	do (verb)
shimemasu	close (verb)
shinai-denwa	local telephone call
shinai-kankō	tour of a city
shinbun	newspaper
shingō	signal
shinguru-rūmu	single room
shinju	pearl
Shinjuku	(place name in Tokyo)
Shinkansen	bullet train
shippō-yaki	cloisonné
shiro	castle
shiseki	historical site
shita	down
shitei-seki	reserved seat
shōchū	distilled spirit usually drunk with water or a mixer
shōji	paper sliding door
shokubutsu-en	botanical garden
shokudō	dining hall
shokudō-sha	dining car
shokuji	meal
shokuji-tsuki	meal included
shoppai	salty
shūgō-jikan	meeting time
shūjitsu	weekday
shūmatsu	weekend

shumi	hobby; interest
shuppatsu-jikan	departure time
sō	so
soba	buckwheat noodles (dark and thin)
soba	nearby
sōbetsu-kai	farewell party
Sō desu.	That's right.
sono	that
sore	that (pronoun)
sōshiki	funeral
soto	out; outside
subarashii	wonderful
sugu	right away
suiden	rice paddy
suika	watermelon
sui-mono	soup (Japanese)
Sui-yōbi	Wednesday
suki	like
suki-yaki	Japanese dish of meat, vegetable, bean curd, etc.
sumi-e	Indian-ink painting
Sumimasen.	Excuse me.
Sumimasen ga...	Sorry, but...
sumō	sumo (traditional Japanese wrestling)
sumoggu	smog
Supein	Spain
Supein-go	Spanish (language)
Supein-jin	Spanish (person)

supōtsu	sport
suppai	sour
sūpu	soup (Western)
supūn	spoon
sushi	vinegared rice and raw fish
sutajiamu	stadium
sutēki	steak
suzushii	cool
tabemasu	eat (verb)
Tai	Thailand
taifū	typhoon
Tai-go	Thai (language)
Taihei-yō	Pacific Ocean
Tai-jin	Thai (person)
taion-kei	thermometer
taishi-kan	embassy
takai	expensive
takenoko	bamboo shoot
tako	octopus
takusan	many; much
takushii-noriba	taxi stand
tamago	egg
tamanegi	onion
tanjō-bi	birthday
tasukemasu	help (verb)
Tasukete!	Help!
te	hand
tearai	restroom
tegami	letter
Teikoku Hoteru	Imperial Hotel

teishoku	set meal
te-nimotsu ichiji azukari-jo	baggage checkroom
tenki	weather
tenki-yohō	weather forecast
tenpura	tempura (Japanese deep-fried food)
tenran-kai	exhibition
tera	Buddhist temple
terebi	television
terefon-kādo	telephone card
tō	pagoda; tower
tō	ten (objects)
tōchaku-jikan	arrival time
tōfu	tofu
tōi	far
tōjiki	chinaware; ceramics
tōka	tenth day of the month
tokei	watch; clock
tokei-ya	watch shop
tokkuri	saké bottle
tokkyū	limited express train
tokkyū-ken	limited express ticket
Tōkyō Eki	Tokyo Station
Tōkyō Tawā	Tokyo Tower
tomarimasu	stop (a car stops)
tomato	tomato
tomemasu	stop (a car)
tomodachi	friend
tōmorokoshi	corn
ton-katsu	pork cutlet
toraberāzu-chekku	traveler's check

toranku	trunk (of a car)
tori	bird
torii	Shinto shrine archway
torimasu	take (verb)
tori-niku	chicken
toshi-totta	old (not young)
tosho-kan	library
totte kudasai	please take
tsuā	tour
tsugi no hi	next day
tsuin	twin room
tsuitachi	first day of the month
tsuke-mono	pickle
tsuki-mi	moon viewing
tsumetai	cold (to the touch)
tsutsumimasu	wrap (verb)
udon	noodles (white and fat)
ue	up
Ueno Kōen	Ueno Park
uisukii	whiskey
uketori	receipt
uketsuke	reception
ukiyo-e	color print of life in old Japan
umi	ocean
una-don	broiled eel and rice
unchin	fare
unchin-hyō	fare table
undō	physical exercise

ushiro	behind
utsukushii	beautiful
wa	(subject particle)
wain	wine
Wakarimasen.	I don't understand.
Wakarimasu.	I understand.
warui	bad
washi	traditional, handmade paper
wasuremasu	forget (verb)
watashi	I
yaki-tori	grilled, skewered chicken
yakkyoku	pharmacy
yakusoku	promise; appointment
yakusoku no jikan	time set for an appointment
yakyū	baseball
yakyū no shiai	baseball game
yama	mountain
yama-nobori	mountain climbing
yasai	vegetable
yasui	inexpensive
yasumi	holiday; day off
yattsu	eight (objects)
yawarakai	soft; tender
yōguruto	yogurt
yōka	eighth day of the month
yokka	fourth day of the month
yoku	well
yomimasu	read (verb)

yon	four
yottsu	four (objects)
yoyaku	reservation
yūbin de dashimasu	mail (a letter)
yūbin-kyoku	post office
yūen-chi	amusement park
yūgata	evening
yuka	floor
yukata	light, cotton kimono
yuki	snow
-yuki	bound for
yukkuri	slowly
yūmei	famous
yu-nomi	teacup
yūran-sen	excursion boat
zaseki shitei-ken	reserved-seat ticket
zasshi	magazine
zeikin	tax
zō	statue